"Many of the great Christian writers down the centuries have set out their theology using the language of 'participation.' Stressing that all things come from God, and that all things find their fulfilment in relation to God, this theology naturally integrates thought, practice, and a common life in the community of the church. Christopher Holmes inhabits this tradition deeply, naturally, and persuasively. His study is particularly notable for the degree to which he is as much at home with the text of the Scriptures as with the writings of the church fathers, Aquinas, or the Reformers."

—**Andrew Davison**, University of Cambridge; author of *Participation in God: A Study in Christian Doctrine and Metaphysics*

"This is a magnificently *theological* reflection on Christian existence. Books about the Christian life often devolve into banal how-to manuals. Here, however, Holmes explores how the life of a Christian opens up to the reality of God himself, in a way that exposes the deepest truths of divine life. In serious but lucid prose, Holmes's skills as a master systematician are movingly deployed in the service of a mind and spirit suffused with the love and adoration of God. Shaped by the classic wisdom of the fathers and of Thomas Aquinas especially, with Scripture at its root, Holmes carefully opens up for the reader the astonishing promise by which God's perfections are shared with us. Dogmatic and spiritual theology are wedded here in an incomparable contemporary fashion that calls for the urgent attention of every Christian, whether student or scholar, lay or ordained."

—**Ephraim Radner**, Wycliffe College

A THEOLOGY OF THE CHRISTIAN LIFE

Imitating and Participating in God

CHRISTOPHER R. J. HOLMES

Baker Academic
a division of Baker Publishing Group
Grand Rapids, Michigan

Published by Baker Academic
a division of Baker Publishing Group
PO Box 6287, Grand Rapids, MI 49516-6287
www.bakeracademic.com

Printed in the United States of America

Library of Congress Cataloging-in-Publication Data
Names: Holmes, Christopher R. J., 1974– author.
Title: A theology of the Christian life : imitating and participating in God / Christopher R. Holmes.
Description: Grand Rapids, Michigan : Baker Academic, a division of Baker Publishing Group, 2021. | Includes index.
Identifiers: LCCN 2021006214 | ISBN 9781540964694 (paperback) | ISBN 9781540964700 (casebound) | ISBN 9781493433384 (ebook)
Subjects: LCSH: Christian life.
Classification: LCC BV4501.3 .H6665 2021 | DDC 248.4—dc23
LC record available at https://lccn.loc.gov/2021006214

Baker Publishing Group publications use paper produced from sustainable forestry practices and post-consumer waste whenever possible.

21   22   23   24   25   26   27   7   6   5   4   3   2   1

To Lillian, Fiona, and Markus

Contents

Acknowledgments   ix

Introduction   xi

Part One ◇◇

1. The Existence of God and the Christian Life   3
   I AM
   How Do We Know That God Exists?
   Spiritual Sight

2. The Manner of God's Existence and the Christian Life   18
   Sense Perception?
   Virtue
   Moses's Example
   Familiarity with God
   The Soul's Elevation in Prayer
   Ascetical Existence
   "The Moral Race Course" of the Baptized

3. Perfection and the Christian Life   43
   The Likeness of God
   Is Christ Perfect?
   Rewards
   The Father's Invisibility
   A Light Yoke

4. Infinity and the Christian Life   62
   Angelic Existence
   The Bodiless God

The Trinitarian Dimension
God as Ever Greater
The Love of God
Devotion and the Doctrine of God
The Perennial Relevance of 1 Corinthians 15:28

5. **Immutability and the Christian Life   81**
Choice
The Way of Life
True Worship
The Unchanging God
On Not Diverging from God
Charity
Friendship with God

Part Two

6. **The Hypostatic Union and the Christian Life   105**
Believing Agency and Being
The Great Difference
Superiority to the Demonic
Living the Divine Life

7. **Virtue and the Christian Life   125**
Virtue
Theological Existence
The Holy Spirit
God's Renown
Prayer

8. **Church and the Christian Life   144**
The One Foundation
A Fruitful Death
The Grace of Prayer

Conclusion   155
Scripture and Ancient Writings Index   161
Author Index   167
Subject Index   169

Acknowledgments

I am grateful to my colleagues in the Theology Programme at the University of Otago. The Programme remains a friendly and hospitable place in which to pursue theology directed toward God for the edification of the faithful. Moreover, the Programme is blessed with some superb PhD students. One of my doctoral students, Brent Rempel, took the time to read the entirely of the manuscript in draft form, offering perceptive comments along the way. I am in his debt.

I am also thankful for my wife Christina and my three children, Lillian (15), Fiona (13), and Markus (8). Lillian, Fiona, and Markus have asked for a while to have a book dedicated to them. Well, this is it. May the truths about which I write empower them, and may God always be their best thought by day and by night.

Introduction

This is a book about the Christian life. It attempts to address the heart of that life by considering some of the great truths concerning God. I interact with many conversation partners, mainly the Greek fathers of the ancient and early medieval church—Origen, Gregory of Nyssa, John of Damascus, and Maximus the Confessor—though Augustine and Thomas Aquinas are never far away.

I have written this book to encourage love of God and reflection on how God's life forms the rubric for imitation of God and participation in him. This book is a scholarly fruit of my reading of a range of (mostly) Greek teachers, written to aid my growth as an expositor and lover of the sacred page, hopefully helping others to do the same. Whether Gregory of Nyssa or Maximus, all these thinkers are united in their adoration of and devotion to the sacred page. Being properly preoccupied with God, they strove prayerfully to speak and write of God in truth.

My basic contention is that God's existence, perfection, infinity, and immutability form a wellspring for Christian life. These "names" (I will discuss the use of this word in chap. 1) function as a template for Christian life. We are Christians when what is true of God is more, rather than less, true of us.

When I first began to think about the book, I thought it would concern Thomas's use of Old Testament Scripture, in the first part of his *Summa Theologiae* (*ST*), dealing with the unity of God's essence. The more I considered the matter, the more I thought the subject too narrow. I have, instead, used Thomas's framework in the first part of my book to offer a thoroughly theocentric account of Christian existence, what Gregory calls the "God-loved life."[1] The second part of the book discusses the impact of God on Christology and ecclesiology.

A twofold scriptural motif anchors the book. The first is imitation. "Be imitators of God," writes Paul (Eph. 5:1). The second is participation. "Thus he has given us . . . his precious and very great promises . . . [so that you] may become participants of the divine nature" (2 Pet. 1:4). Both themes help us to consider how we might resemble the God in whom we exist.

The pages to come unfold a program of spiritual renewal founded on some of the essential names or attributes of the divine being. I describe something of the personal, moral, and spiritual import of God "as He is in Himself."[2] Though the emphasis of sacred doctrine "is more theoretical [*speculativa*] than practical," sacred doctrine is not indifferent to human acts.[3] Instead, sacred doctrine as "theoretical in one respect and practical in another" considers "human acts only in so far as they prepare men for that achieved knowledge of God on which their eternal bliss reposes."[4] In this book, I unite the contemplative and the practical. I offer a scripturally charged account of some of God's essential names with a view to imitation of and participation in God. In other words, my concern with these attributes is descriptive and prescriptive. What do they say about God's being, and what kind of life do they encourage?

1. Gregory of Nyssa, *On the Christian Mode of Life*, in *Ascetical Works*, trans. Virginia Woods Callahan, Fathers of the Church (Washington, DC: Catholic University of America Press, 1967), 152.

2. Thomas Aquinas, *Summa Theologiae* (hereafter *ST*) I.2, trans. Blackfriars (London: Eyre & Spottiswoode, 1964), 2:3.

3. Aquinas, *ST* I.1.4, in *Basic Writings of Saint Thomas Aquinas*, ed. Anton C. Pegis, vol. 1, *God and the Order of Creation* (Indianapolis: Hackett, 1997), 9. The Latin *speculativa* can also be rendered "contemplative." Such a translation is more fitting for my purposes.

4. *ST* I.1.5 (trans. Blackfriars, 1:17–19), I.1.4 (1:17).

The Centrality of Scripture

Scripture is central to the undertaking of writing this book. Scripture determines whether what the church proclaims is true about God. It also encourages the believing community to think of how claims regarding God's nature, substance, and essence determine Christian life. Not surprisingly, Thomas opens his *Summa* by quoting 2 Timothy 3:16–17: "All scripture is inspired by God and is useful for teaching, for reproof, for correction, and for training in righteousness, so that everyone who belongs to God may be proficient, equipped for every good work."[5] As we begin the book, we need to clarify Scripture's particular function, following 2 Timothy. Scripture teaches us about God, and it leads us on the journey to abundant life because Scripture belongs to God.

Let us consider for a moment how God uses Scripture. Thomas writes, "The Holy Scriptures are the way to salvation," and that in three ways. "He [the author of 2 Timothy] commends Scripture by reason of its principle, by reason of its profitable effect, and by reason of its ultimate fruit and success."[6]

We have Scripture because God, its principle, exists. Scripture is "from God" (2 Pet. 1:21). When we receive Scripture in faith, we receive God's voice. Extracanonical writings instruct "mediately" (indirectly), whereas God instructs our understanding "immediately [directly] through the Sacred Scriptures."[7] Scripture always has priority, however, as Thomas argues, because of its immediacy to God. Therein lies its uniqueness and authority. No other collection of writings is God's in the sense that Scripture is. When we draw near to Scripture, we draw near to God.

The effects of Scripture's immediacy to God are twofold. Scripture "teaches man to know the truth and persuades him to work justice."[8] As Thomas explains, sacred doctrine's "chief aim" is to teach about God, who is truth itself, and to teach that God is "the beginning and

5. *ST* I.1.1, s.c. (trans. Blackfriars, 1:7).
6. Thomas Aquinas, *Commentaries on 2 Timothy* §124, commenting on 2 Timothy 3:16, in *Commentaries on St. Paul's Epistles to Timothy, Titus, and Philemon*, trans. Chrysostom Baer (South Bend, IN: St. Augustine's Press, 2007), 136.
7. Aquinas, *Commentaries on St. Paul's Epistles* §125.
8. Aquinas, *Commentaries on St. Paul's Epistles* §127.

end of all things and of reasoning creatures especially."[9] Scripture teaches the truth, and at the same time it persuades us to mind the truth. The former highlights its speculative character, the latter its practical character. Scripture commends God. Scripture also commends human works that commend God. Scripture encourages us to live a life transparent to God, a life in truth that works justice.

In the chapters ahead, I follow Thomas's lead. I communicate something of God's grandeur, and suggest how his creatures can imitate and participate in that grandeur. Accordingly, this book is both speculative and practical. Speculative reason's subject matter is God, and practical reason's subject matter is human action in reference to God. Each has different concerns, to be sure, but these "two things are necessary" to reason.[10] Each must endeavor to know God and in so doing refute errors contrary to God and what God wills.

Scripture's immediacy to God means many things. Most importantly, Scripture teaches and persuades like no other. The Spirit breathes Scripture. Scripture instructs and convinces, not on its own steam but because of the Paraclete spoken of, for example, in John 14:26 and 15:26. Scripture's authority derives from its source—the truth. All talk of Scripture's nature has to do with the possessive phrase "of God." Scripture teaches about God and refutes those things that are contrary to God because its source is God himself.

We pay attention to Scripture because there is little else in this life more immediate to God than Scripture. The effects of Holy Scripture are great, and my calling as a theologian is to encourage others to lovingly contemplate those effects. Scripture is sufficient, lacking nothing. Scripture teaches the truth, which is God, and thereby reproves falsity; but Scripture's function is not simply pedagogical. Scripture liberates. As Thomas says, Scripture is able to "free one from evil and lead him to the good."[11] I want to capture something of the sense of its liberating and leading ministry, especially as it instructs us in God and our imitation of him.

This book explores how we might imitate God's existence, his manner of existence, his perfection, infinity, and immutability. We are

9. *ST* I.1.2 (trans. Blackfriars, 2:3).
10. Aquinas, *Commentaries on St. Paul's Epistles* §127.
11. Aquinas, *Commentaries on St. Paul's Epistles* §127.

on holy ground in treating the God of whom Scripture speaks. The endeavor requires reliance on Lady Wisdom herself. Lady Wisdom gives us, following Wisdom of Solomon 10:10, "knowledge of holy things." We begin our inquiry, then, with open hands. Sacred doctrine invites us to consider things "divinely revealed." Lady Wisdom calls from "the highest places in the town" (Prov. 9:3). Those who consider God are made wise and discerning by the one whom they consider and imitate.[12] This inquiry is indeed an exercise in wisdom (see *ST* I.1.6) because it concerns the wise architect, God himself.

But acquiring wisdom is not an end in itself. As Thomas's appeal to Titus 1:9 in *ST* I.1.8 demonstrates, we, as those being made wise, are to exalt in what is true and convince others of its truthfulness. Therefore, wisdom and its pursuit have a regulative function. The wise "preach with sound doctrine" and "refute those who contradict it."[13] Hence, the treatment of God that follows is intended not only to assist those who preach but also to correct those—really all of us—who are tempted to live with less than God.

Scripture meets us where we are by using "corporeal things" to expound "spiritual truths."[14] Scripture has many senses, as Hebrews 10:1, cited by Thomas in *ST* I.10, reminds us. But we must not be preoccupied with things that are shadows. We must deal with realities. Since Thomas's great work is so preoccupied with Scripture and its author, who is God, surely we are also not mistaken in being preoccupied with Scripture. We preoccupy ourselves with Scripture that we might be preoccupied with God. We do so in order to hear about God as he is and to learn what is essential to the three persons. What is essential to Father, Son, and Holy Spirit functions as the motor for Christian life.

The Basic Outline

I use the following names and topics as a rough template for the first section of the book: existence (chap. 1) and the manner of God's

12. *ST* I.1.3 (trans. Pegis 1:8).
13. *ST* I.1.8 (trans. Blackfriars, 1:29).
14. *ST* I.9 (trans. Pegis, 15).

existence (chap. 2), perfection (chap. 3), infinity (chap. 4), and immutability (chap. 5). These names are common to the Father, Son, and Spirit, though uniquely proper to each; they are convertible with their one essence, and we are called to imitate the names as we are called to exist as God does. Perfection is a dominical command (see Matt. 5:48). We share as creatures in the gift of (relative) infinity. We are made immutable in and through Jesus Christ. God communicates his unity to us in order that we might be his likeness, not in an absolute but in a relative sense.

In chapter 6, I explore how these names designated above shape our christological thinking, especially concerning the unity of divinity and humanity in the one person of the Son. I then consider how the hypostatic union informs Christian life. In chapter 7, I explore the impact of these names on our thinking about the church. In chapter 8, I articulate something of the intensely personal dimension of teaching about God and the importance of how we speak of the one Lord God.

Scripture is at the forefront throughout the book. Psalm 53:1 and John 4:24 anchor my account of God's existence and the manner of his existence. Matthew 5:48 is the center of my discussion of perfection, while Jeremiah 23:24 grounds the treatment of infinity, and Malachi 3:6 immutability. Thomas cites these passages in his treatment of the same subject matter in the first part of the *Summa Theologiae*. We shall see, as we consider these texts, Scripture's ability to communicate the truth about God. We shall also see how all these attributes are communicable. In keeping with our thesis, the names determine and shape Christian life. The doctrine of God is fertile ground for Christian life. Though of course matters of Christian life are, in terms of doctrinal architecture, downstream of the doctrine of God, the Christian life is never far behind. I write this book in a personal voice that I trust is not wholly inadequate to convey deeply metaphysical truths.

Why This Book and Why Now?

This book has provided me with an occasion to read and reflect on figures in the Christian tradition hitherto largely unknown to me. I have sensed for some time the need to write a book on the Christian life firmly rooted in theology proper, indeed as an exercise in theology proper. I pursue the Lord with an unashamedly personal, doxological, and prayerful voice. Over the course of the last decade or so, I have come to appreciate that the mode of communicating theological truth and the message communicated are inseparable. A devotional frame is appropriate to unfolding some of the riches of God's being. It is important to connect our reflections on Scripture with tracts of Christian teaching that are not always adequately integrated into our Christian faith traditions. When one reads Anselm's *Proslogion*, one learns to pray even as one learns about God. We learn about God by praying.

The doctrine of God, of the one divine essence, is fertile ground for imitation. We imitate what we know and love, the Trinity. "Be imitators of God." And so, what follows is a program for spiritual renewal in relation to God. It is about seeing the Christian life in utterly theocentric terms, for conceiving Christian life as a pilgrimage toward ever greater likeness to God in and through Jesus Christ in order that his Father, our Father, might, in the Spirit, be "all in all" (1 Cor. 15:28).

Part One

1

The Existence of God and the Christian Life

Fools say in their hearts, "There is no God."

—Psalm 53:1

God exists. This is where we begin our spiritual journey. God's existence is our first step toward imitating and participating in God. Let us think about this. Our pilgrimage begins with God, the reality of his existence. And it will finish with God, seeing him face to face. God is our beginning, middle, and end. God exists, and on this basis God speaks, communicates, and reveals himself to us in order that we might love him and, in turn, enjoy him.

Existence, in the case of God, is a name. We mean by this that existence is not a quality of God. Rather, existence is God himself. Existence is a name for being, not an inert conceptual property of being.[1] God shows himself to be one who, following Gregory of

---

1. This is David Bentley Hart's point. He blames Plato for not enduring "the mystery of these *names* for being, and soon had to begin to substitute for them the inert conceptual *properties* of being." David Bentley Hart, *The Hidden and the Manifest: Essays in Theology and Metaphysics* (Grand Rapids: Eerdmans, 2017), 6.

Nyssa, "possesses existence in [his] own nature."[2] Existence is a divine name, meaning that God is existence itself; existence is supremely true of God.

This work considers existence (a name) as a first priority, even in advance of love and power, because this is where Scripture begins. Scripture teaches us that God is the highest cause of all things.[3] Our treatment of God and the shape of life in relation to God rest on an understanding of God as the cause of our existence. Because God exists in and of himself, he is able to grant existence to what is not himself. God creates. The narrative pattern of Scripture begins there. God causes things other than himself to exist. Because of God, there is something rather than nothing. And God needs no other thing in order to be, for God just is. Summarizing Martin Heidegger, David Bentley Hart puts it this way: "Nothing that is (including becoming) is able to account for itself."[4]

To speak of God in this way is not a "natural" way of thinking. We are not contemplating God in a way that is independent of divine revelation in scriptural form. We are beholden to scriptural truth. Scripture summons us to confess God as the highest cause. Description of God as "the highest cause" (*altissima causa*) and as "deepest origin and highest end" is indicative of truths that exceed human reason without being contrary to it. Indeed, this is true of all matters pertaining to sacred doctrine, and not just the matter of recognizing God as our origin and end. Thinking about God in causal terms under the tutelage of the Scriptures means that we affirm God's existence and that we recognize him as the great "I AM" of Exodus 3:14, the one who causes all things.[5]

2. Gregory of Nyssa, *The Life of Moses* 2.23, trans. Abraham J. Malherbe and Everett Ferguson (New York: Paulist Press, 1978), 60.

3. Thomas Aquinas, *Summa Theologiae* (hereafter *ST*) I.6, in *Basic Writings of Saint Thomas Aquinas*, ed. Anton C. Pegis, vol. 1, *God and the Order of Creation* (Indianapolis: Hackett, 1997), 11. The Blackfriars translation—the enterprise of Dominicans from English-speaking provinces of the order and of their friends—runs thus: "Now holy teaching goes to God most personally as deepest origin and highest end."

4. Hart, *The Hidden and the Manifest*, 16. In this regard, John writes, "All things came into being through him, and without him not one thing came into being" (John 1:3).

5. Thomas cites this text in *ST* I.2.3, s.c.

We know God exists because of what God has made, following Romans 1:20.[6] Creation's origin and end of things—the technical Thomistic term is "effects," whether of nature or of grace—is God, and the truth of our existence lies in God. Created things announce that they are made. They bear the likeness of their Creator. Even more, they "participate in manifold ways in that which is one in God."[7] Because created things participate in their cause, they are the means through which we understand God.

Recall that God is unseen (John 1:18). We cannot see God's essence "as it is in itself one."[8] Such uninterrupted seeing is for the life of the world to come. But we can, through created things, take "the first step towards understanding it [God's essence]."[9] The first attribute we derive from visible created things is that of existence. We proceed "from the features of the existence of the world [to] the principles of the world."[10] The features of the world manifest their ground—existence itself—and they do so naturally.

God knows himself to be existence itself, and God "discloses [this] for others to share."[11] Existence is convertible with God. God exists in relation to himself and is not caused by something outside himself. When we say God, we say the name existence. We indicate thereby that God is self-existent, needing nothing outside himself in order to be. Even more, God causes things whose existence lies in himself.

There is a crucial distinction at work here, and it is heuristic. We are talking about the distinction between existence (the *that* of God) and essence (the *what* of God). Visible things give us understanding of God, that God is. But they do not enable us "to know him comprehensively for what he is."[12] In scriptural terms, "no one has ever seen God" (John 1:18), and so we, on this side of glory, do not know him in a direct sense. This eschatological reserve is at work

6. Thomas cites this text in *ST* I.2.2, s.c.
7. Thomas Aquinas, *Commentary on Romans* 1.6.117, commenting on Rom. 1:20, available at https://aquinas.cc/199/en/~Rom.
8. Thomas Aquinas, *Commentary on Romans* 1.6.117, commenting on Rom. 1:20, trans. Fabian R. Larcher, OP (Steubenville, OH: Emmaus Academic, 2020), 41.
9. *ST* I.2.2, s.c. (trans. Blackfriars, 2:9).
10. Hart, *The Hidden and the Manifest*, 23.
11. *ST* I.6 (trans. Blackfriars, 1:23).
12. *ST* I.2.2, ad. 3 (trans. Blackfriars, 2:11).

from the start. We know God to be identical with his goodness, life, and power, for example, but we do not know how. That is for heaven. In this life, we speak and sing of God's existence, recognizing the inadequacy of what we voice. That said, a discourse that takes the form of "worship, prayer, and rejoicing" is less inadequate than any other—hence the form that this book takes.[13]

I AM

The first Scripture Thomas cites in his treatment of the self-evident character of God's existence is, not surprisingly, Psalm 53:1.[14] It is a foolish thing to say that there is no God because it goes against reality itself. All things exist in relation to God. The key to avoiding foolishness and thus to becoming wise is to recognize that God exists and exists otherwise than we do. For example, God is not capable of either doing or saying anything that is false, whereas we are. Though God's effects demonstrate God's existence, we can and often do ignore their testimony, and that is because we are, frequently, foolish. Our foolishness, however, does not obviate, entirely, the witness of created things to God. That is why the fool speaks only to himself—in his heart. The fool denies his creatureliness. He ignores the Creator-creature distinction. The fool exists, therefore, in gross violation of the first commandment.

The first step toward genuine Christian existence is to acknowledge God's existence. Scripture starts with the twofold assumption that God exists and reveals himself. Neither God's existence nor God's speech is without effect. This is in contradiction to the fool's speech. It has no power, whereas God's word comes about—"Let there be . . ." The fool's judgments regarding God are false. He treats fallible human reason as if it were infallible. He speaks in relation to himself and not God. He is like the one who builds on sand, thinking sand is as stable as rock (see Matt. 7:24–27; Luke 6:47–49). The fool ignores the Book of Nature and thus is indifferent and even hostile toward the Scriptures.

13. Hart, *The Hidden and the Manifest*, 27.
14. *ST* I.2.1, s.c. (trans. Blackfriars, 2:5–7).

The Scriptures, especially the Old Testament Scriptures, delight in recording how God speaks through created things. A donkey—Balaam's—speaks God's message; the heavens declare God's majesty; prophets like Jeremiah declare searing words from the Lord to stubborn kings. Created things, incarnate and discarnate, animals, humans, to say nothing of angels, speak words that are not their own but from the Lord God. When they do so, their words have effect; they do not come back empty, for they bear the Lord's voice (see Isa. 55:11).

Accordingly, it is fitting to begin treatment of the Christian life with God's existence. This name above all others instructs us in the nature of the relationship between the created and uncreated.[15] This relationship, we discover, is a participatory one. For example, God is life. Life belongs to God, and life, whether it be human or the life of living things such as trees, exists only in relation to God. God is life, and the lives of creatures have a certain likeness to God insofar as the life they have is a participation in God. Created things (works of nature) as well as supernatural things (works of grace) participate in their cause. The same is true of creatures' goodness. Life and goodness are true of creatures. To be a creature is to participate "in that which is one in God."[16]

We exist and God exists, but there is always a great dissimilarity between God's mode of existence and our own.[17] God is supereminent. Existence is not something common to both God and us, as if existence were outside and beyond God. Thomas's treatment of God's one essence, as we shall see, is satisfying, biblically speaking,

15. John Behr notes that with respect to Origen's *On First Principles*, "the distinction between the uncreated and the created finds its place within his overarching apostolic distinction between the seen and transient, on the one hand, and the unseen and eternal, on the other." Introduction to Origen, *On First Principles*, ed. and trans. John Behr (Oxford: Oxford University Press, 2017), 1:xliv. Behr argues that the distinction between the created and uncreated is basic to the later tradition, though not basic to Origen. I am thankful to Behr for a treatment of Origen encouraging renewed attention to 2 Cor. 4:18.

16. Aquinas, *Commentary on Romans* 1.6.117, commenting on Rom. 1:20 (trans. Larcher, 41).

17. See further Erich Przywara's magisterial treatment in Erich Przywara, *Analogia Entis: Metaphysics—Original Structure and Universal Rhythm*, trans. John R. Betz and David Bentley Hart (Grand Rapid: Eerdmans, 2014).

because it recognizes how the two books given to us by God—nature and scriptural revelation—are compatible with each other. Though there are profound differences between the two—Scripture interprets the former—we see that created things speak of the existence of their Creator, just as Scripture reveals knowledge of the inner nature of their Creator.

The fool cannot receive invisible truth communicated by Scripture because he cannot accept the testimony of visible things—"Look at the birds," says Jesus (Matt. 6:26). That is why the fool can only *say*, not *effect*, something. The fool has no reality; his speech is grounded in nothing and has no power. But God's speech brings about that of which he speaks. "Let there be light" (Gen. 1:3). God's speech is creative and at the same time revelatory of himself, whereas the fool's speech can only reside in himself. It has neither creative power nor revelatory power concerning truth.

How do we avoid foolishness in favor of the great I AM? What kind of moral and spiritual program is necessary to speak of God as self-subsisting, as one for whom existence is not an attribute but a noun? How may we imitate the great I AM? The reason the fool is mistaken as to God's existence is that his heart is cold and his soul callous. Lack of virtue and piety—that is the problem. In this chapter (as with the book as a whole) I describe the kind of piety appropriate to an understanding of God as one who exists.

There is another way to put this: The fool's problems are not only intellectual. They are also spiritual and moral. It is because he is wicked that he does not believe that God exists. His wickedness and ungodliness, to use Paul's language from Romans 1:18, prevent him from knowing what exists in and of itself and is good by nature. Because the fool does not know what is good, he desires neither to participate in it nor to imitate it. The same, however, is not true of the wise man. As Gregory notes, "Those who know what is good by nature [i.e., God] desire participation in it."[18] Those who are virtuous will not entertain improper notions about God's nature, as does the fool.

Our journey in this life is (hopefully) toward purity. Without purity of heart, it is impossible to speak truthfully of God. Our journey is

18. Gregory of Nyssa, *Life of Moses* 1.7.

also a journey into true creatureliness. God's names structure how we think about our creatureliness in relation to God.[19] Thomas knows this, and this is why his program is so attentive to *how* we speak of divine things. As we grow in reverence for God, we put foolish things behind. We become wise; we exist in a way that is more, rather than less, Godlike. We stop thinking of God as mutable and subject to passions and whims. We long, instead, to imitate God, to be like him, impassible, steadfast, and faithful.

The fool is not worthy of God because the fool is wedded to himself and his own opinions. He thinks things that are false because he thinks himself the measure of all things. Virtue and proper notions of God are always directly related. The predominance of Old Testament wisdom texts in *ST* I.1 reminds us that proper notions about the divine nature—sacred doctrine's concern—are an intellectual fruit of reverence. If we hide from the truth of our creatureliness, we will think and say things that are false.

Thomas's comments on Psalms 53:1 in his Psalms commentary are particularly apt. Thomas reminds us that sinners love sin; hence the designation wicked. Their wickedness, he says, comes "from the contempt for God." The primary fruit of foolishness is hostility toward God, which is the fruit of denying one's creatureliness. The wise, however, do not hold God in contempt, "for wisdom has to do with divine cognition."[20] Wisdom knows God as God exists—that is, as one who exists in and through himself. The wise person knows herself to be created. She sees herself as a participation in existence itself, dependent on God—who is existence itself.

Thomas's discussion of Psalm 53 is also helpful and worth brief exploration. Thomas cites Anselm—"nobody is capable of thinking God not to be"—as a platform for discussing "two ways in which something can be unknown to us. In one way, on its own account, in the other way, with respect to us." In terms of the first, Thomas has in mind "things that are unknown to us that are foremost with respect to being, like contingency, prime matter, motion, and time." In terms of the second way, he has in mind "those things [that] are

---

19. See further Hart, *The Hidden and the Manifest*, 42.
20. Thomas Aquinas, *Commentary on the Psalms* 52, trans. Gregory Sadler, available at http://hosted.desales.edu/w4/philtheo/loughlin/ATP/Psalm_52.html.

unknown to us that excel our cognition." This refers to God. Thomas continues, "I say therefore that if we consider God in Himself, he cannot be thought not to be." It is, in other words, impossible to conceive of God as not existing—"no proposition is better known than that one whose predicate is included in the subject." When we say "God is," we say something that is true with respect to God himself. Existence is true of God himself, as God is existence itself. However, God's being—God's essence—"is not known to us, but it becomes known to us by effects."[21] We know God, in the pure act of being that he is, via his effects.

The fool who denies God does so in the face of "any effects of God whatsoever," whether they be either God's providential workings or miracles. The fool also denies his heart, since what God is "is in the heart from God [by God's agency]," and the fool "chooses none of this." The fool is, as a result, corrupted. He becomes prey to "the heat of lust and fear";[22] his life becomes devoid of good. For the Christian, however, the love of God is concomitant with good works. God knows those who do good, but God is displeased with the fool. There is little in the fool that is of God, and so more and more in himself that is against God.

How Do We Know That God Exists?

It is worth pausing, for a moment, to consider how we know of God's existence. In his remarkable discussion of Romans 1:20, Thomas says that we cannot know "what God is," citing the inscription in Acts 17:23: "*to the unknown God.*" We cannot know God's whatness because our "knowledge begins with things connatural to him [i.e., us, humankind], namely, sensible creatures, which are not proportioned to representing the divine essence."[23] The divine essence is invisible, and so cannot be represented by the sensible. The divine essence—the "what" of God—is unknowable because of the extent to which God supersedes "sensible creatures." This is not a counsel for despair, however; just because we know in a creaturely—that is,

21. Aquinas, *Commentary on the Psalms* 52.
22. Aquinas, *Commentary on the Psalms* 52.
23. Aquinas, *Commentary on Romans* 1.6.114, commenting on Rom. 1:20.

sensible—way does not mean that we cannot know God at all. We know God in a way befitting our creatureliness.

Thomas continues: we are "capable of knowing God from such [sensible] creatures in three ways, . . . first of all through causality." Created things have an "unchangeable and unfailing principle," and that is God. In knowing God through what God causes, "it can be known that God exists." We know that God exists because God causes things other than God. Second, God "can be known by the way of excellence." Though God is "a common and exceeding cause," God's excellence is shown in that he "is above all things" that he causes. God does not exist alongside what he creates. God exists, rather, as one who is above what he creates. God completely exceeds created things, even as he gives them a share in his existence. Third and last, God "can be known by the way of negation." Because God's existence exceeds what he causes, "nothing in creatures can belong to him," for "God is unchangeable and infinite."[24] Accordingly, God does not exist as we do. Our life is a participation in the life of God, whereas the reverse is not true.

Two of Thomas's intentions in describing the nature of our knowledge of God's existence are particularly relevant to our discussion. First, the three ways of knowing agree with the light of reason. There is nothing unreasonable about affirming God's existence in the manner sketched above. Though we cannot see what God is, we can be lead to God through the light of reason. Such light does not contradict the light of faith, though the light of faith utterly exceeds reason. Second, denying God's existence is (again) foolishness. Unbelief contradicts the light of reason. It goes against the very grain of existence, which is caused by God himself. Unbelief has no ground and is absurd. Therefore, unbelief is profoundly immoral; it discourages a life of "innocence" that leads to the "divine image."[25] This is the kind of thinking behind Paul's statements in Romans 3:9–20, especially verse 10, which is a paraphrase of Ecclesiastes 7:20. Unbelief is unreasonable *and* immoral, denoting a state that degrades our humanity, leading us away from God.

24. Aquinas, *Commentary on Romans* 1.6.115, commenting on Rom. 1:20.
25. Aquinas, *Commentary on the Psalms* 52.

Being a human being is a moral undertaking. The same goes for being a Christian. Human existence involves "in every moment . . . always a moment of judgment." The fool forgets this and refuses "to love all things in the love of God."[26] When the fool says there is no God, he does not speak out of ignorance. Instead, as Thomas notes in his commentary on Romans 1:20, ignorance of God proceeds from guilt, which leads to vanity. Fools are foolish because they have failed to worship God. The fool denies that God exists because he does not give thanks to God as the cause of all that is good. The creaturely correlate of acknowledging God's existence is worship. Foolishness is a fruit of the denial of one's creatureliness. Were the fool to be thankful, he would believe. Were he to lean on God, his thinking would be less futile.

Surprising though it may seem, there is an eschatological dimension to thinking about God's existence. God's existence is one with himself, just as God's goodness and power are one in and with himself. However, things will be different in heaven. Not that God will be different—of course!—but that we will know God differently. Our knowing will be complete. Knowledge will give way to sight. We will see the eternal God, "the ultimate end unto which all things tend."[27] God's essence will be "known to us in regard to what it is."[28]

Foolishness ends, as far as this life is concerned, in exhaustion. The fool contends against the grain of his creatureliness. He resists God, toward whom all things move. The fool lacks patience and, with that, humility. He assumes that the unseen is unreal. He cannot accept that knowing and loving are modes of seeing. The fool's existence is entropic, the denial of "the common good in which all things participate."[29] This is tragic. As Gregory writes, those "who do not acknowledge God . . . are delivered up to shameful affections."[30]

Following Ephesians 4:23, the fool needs a renewal of "the spirit of your minds." He must turn to Scripture. In embracing "spiritual contemplation" of Scripture, we become less foolish. As Gregory

26. Hart, *The Hidden and the Manifest*, 39.
27. Hart, *The Hidden and the Manifest*, 37.
28. Aquinas, *Commentary on Romans* 1.6.117, commenting on Rom. 1:20.
29. Aquinas, *Commentary on Romans* 1.6.117, commenting on Rom. 1:20.
30. Gregory of Nyssa, *Life of Moses* 2.76.

says, spiritual contemplation of "scripture leads our understanding upward to the higher levels of virtue."[31] Virtue—purity of heart—is necessary for contemplation of God, for recognizing God as God is. Without Scripture, we lack the means God uses to correct our foolishness. As we contemplate Scripture, we learn the character of God's existence and the extent to which God's existence is unlike our own. God is not double-minded, to say nothing of being foolish. The wise person speaks of God in ways commensurate with God.

A wise and pure form of life "pertains to the Divine." As Gregory writes, the two sides of virtues are both "[learning] the things which must be known about God" and "learning by what pursuits the virtuous life is perfected."[32] Virtue involves knowing God and the modes of life that encourage such knowledge. Scripture thus aids virtue. Its literal sense is not isolated from the spiritual; the literal has a spiritual meaning. The spiritual meaning "agrees with the literal account."[33] The literal yields to the spiritual, whether we are talking about Scripture or visible things in general. The fool does not understand the interpretation either of the Book of Nature or the Scriptures. The proper interpretation is possible only if we have been "striving toward virtue."[34] God assists the understanding of those who are virtuous, helping them to see that all things exist in relation to himself.

Spiritual Sight

God's effects attest their cause. Fools deny, as Gregory notes, "the secret and ineffable areas of the intelligence."[35] Conscience, following Romans 2:15, is among those areas. Fools deny God's exterior and interior witness to his existence.

Virtue—as the fruit of good works—and belief go together. Without virtue, we lack faith and "conscience toward life."[36] The lack of a "conscience toward life" encourages the nihilism that is rampant

31. Gregory of Nyssa, *Life of Moses* 2.152.
32. Gregory of Nyssa, *Life of Moses* 2.166.
33. Gregory of Nyssa, *Life of Moses* 2.217.
34. Gregory of Nyssa, *Life of Moses* 2.49.
35. Gregory of Nyssa, *Life of Moses* 2.188.
36. Gregory of Nyssa, *Life of Moses* 2.192.

today. Nihilism cannot see what is beautiful; the nihilistic mind is dark, unable to see excellence, unable to see "what is beyond"— namely, God. Nihilism's end is death—nonexistence. Unbelief and the nihilism it encourages—foolishness, really—lacks the desire for anything good, collapsing in on itself. Sloth is the fruit of the fool's denial. The wise person, however, sees the invisible in the visible, existence itself reflected in creaturely goodness. Remarkably, the fool does not deny that God cannot be known. His judgment is more basic. God is nonexistent, the fool says. He "has turned from true Being to what he considers by sense perception to have being."[37] The only thing that has true being for the fool is himself. The fool thinks that God is some thing among other things to be known (or denied). The fool, in his foolishness, does not turn to God, whose "nature is to transcend all characteristics."[38] Existence is not a characteristic. More than that, existence is God himself. God is I AM.

The more we long for God and the greater our sincerity in confessing God, the greater is the intensity of our existence. To exist is to long for God. The more keen the desire for God, the sincerer our imitation of God. The more we grow into our creatureliness, the more we honor the difference between God and ourselves. We are created; God is not. Just as the fool's denial of God leads to his diminishment, so does our imitation of God lead to flourishing and increase.

The burden of this book is to unfold glimpses of the biblical testimony to God's essential names, names which give rise to an overtly ascetical mode of life. The fool is not ascetically inclined, because he judges good with reference to himself. As a result, he does not discover what is truly good. He can neither see nor do good because his existence is self-enclosed. Self-control, humility—these things are not part of his vocabulary.

In contemplating God's existence, we begin where Moses began. Moses did not begin shepherding the people of God with a face-to-face encounter with God. Instead, he was confronted by a voice speaking through a burning bush. His task was to follow God's terrifying voice, which he did. Moses made progress in hearing God's voice and eventually experienced God's coming to him "in a dense

37. Gregory of Nyssa, *Life of Moses* 2.234.
38. Gregory of Nyssa, *Life of Moses* 2.234.

cloud, in order that the people may hear when I speak with you and so trust you ever after" (Exod. 19:9). Moses, in time, became God's friend (see Exod. 33:11). Few of us on this side of glory will enjoy such intimacy with God. However, we can aim, as Gregory notes, "to be called servants of God by virtue of the lives we live."[39]

As we advance in the highest virtues—faith, hope, and love—we bear some of the "distinguishing marks" of the divine character in ourselves. We begin to exist in likeness to God, in a Godlike way. God, the One Who Is, exists, and this God shares with us his existence, his essence in the pure act of being that he is.[40] We begin to live in a participatory manner, using existence as our starting point, just as Scripture does. Once there was nothing, and now there is something, all because of God.

As we contemplate Moses's life, we see the twofold revelation of God's name. First is the signification of the divine nature, "I AM WHO I AM" (Exod. 3:14). This is not a personal name. Rather, it pertains to God's essence, which is existence itself. This is God's *proper* name. The further revelation is that God says to Moses that he is "the LORD, the God of your ancestors" (Exod. 3:15). The divine name is "two names."[41]

Following Thomas, we begin with existence. The intention is to describe the One Who Is, who is existence itself, personally as the Lord. The metaphysical and the personal "support" each other.[42] This is why the treatment that follows moves seamlessly between the Old Testament and the New Testament. There is one God: the Lord God who speaks to Moses and who was born of the virgin.

Herein we see the Christian life coming into focus. Divine names like "existence" encourage "conformity to the archetype."[43] We are called to imitate and conform to the divine names. With God as our helper, we bear in ourselves, by grace, the glimpses of the distinguishing marks of the I AM. We become more real rather than less, more ourselves as creatures, when we submit to the One Who Is, whose

39. Gregory of Nyssa, *Life of Moses* 2.315.
40. Thomas Joseph White, *Exodus* (Grand Rapids: Brazos, 2016), 42.
41. White, *Exodus*, 39.
42. White, *Exodus*, 294.
43. Gregory of Nyssa, *Life of Moses* 2.318.

essence it is to exist. We want "to be known by God and to become his friend."[44] We become his friend insofar as we resemble him. God is friendly to those in whom there is more rather than less of him, those whose lives are coincident with his. What is true of God—of the three, of the being common to them—is true of us in a relative sense when we become God's friend. We become truly human. We are not displaced but healed.

When we think about the personal name of God, the Lord, we see how we may become friendly with God. The Lord speaks to Moses and makes Moses and his people his own, suffering their infidelity while remaining faithful and ultimately destroying hard-heartedness on the cross. Gregory calls us to the "spiritual interpretation of the things spoken literally."[45] I engage in this spiritual interpretation of Scripture with a view to Christian life, an exercise in transferring to our lives "what is contemplated." "Becoming God's friend [is] the only thing worthy of honor and desire."[46] We consider what God is, and how God conforms us to his archetype, and all that through the ultimate, once-and-for-all revelation of his personal name, the Lord Jesus Christ.

Conclusion

God bears the name existence, manifest in his revelation to Moses as the great I AM. A fitting home for imitation of God is the general, the names common to the three persons. God would have us be like him and act like him. In considering the existence of God as pure act, we encounter one who, because he is existence itself, is entirely actual. The wise person participates in God's existence, loving rather than denying him. She exists in likeness to God. Accordingly, consideration of God's existence provides us with our first window into Christian life, understood in theocentric terms. In contradistinction to the actions of the fool, such a life begins with acknowledging that God exists. Existence is archetypal, as are the other names we will

44. Gregory of Nyssa, *Life of Moses* 2.320.
45. Gregory of Nyssa, *Life of Moses* 2.320.
46. Gregory of Nyssa, *Life of Moses* 2.320.

explore. The manner of God's existence provides fertile ground for conceiving of life in relationship with him.

In thinking diligently about the manner of God's existence, we believe that he exists, but we know not the manner in which he exists. The dissimilarity between Creator and creature is always greater than the similarity. Nonetheless, as we acknowledge God and begin to love and thank him for the gift of existence, we become like him. We recognize that the life we have and the life of the whole created order is not proper to us but proper to him. A God-loved life begins with God. God exists—I AM. The Lord longs to render us intimate with and capable of walking in his company.

2

The Manner of God's Existence and the Christian Life

God is spirit.

—John 4:24

This chapter attends to how teaching on God's manner of his existence—his incorporeality and simplicity—informs Christian life. With the aid of Maximus the Confessor and Gregory of Nyssa, we draw out the ascetical import of divine simplicity for the Christian life. Pressing questions are thereby raised: If the manner of God's existence is incorporeal and simple—that is, free of composition—how are we to imitate him? What kind of virtue is appropriate to God, who is unseen and simple? Does imitation of the incorporeal lead to the denigration or exaltation of the corporeal? What might it mean to participate in the manner of God's existence?

As we pursue this point, we are always mindful of the dangers of idolatry. Meditation upon God's existence overcomes our idolatrous tendencies. God is being itself; his name is existence—I AM. God has being, unlike idols, which "are those things that seem to have being in the vain opinion of men."[1] We begin by considering how we may be

---

1. Gregory of Nyssa, *Treatise on the Inscriptions of the Psalms* 1.4.28, trans. Ronald E. Heine (Oxford: Clarendon, 1995), 93.

said to imitate one who is unseen and simple. We contemplate how we may grow in likeness to the manner of God's existence in order that a share in and participation of God's blessedness may be our own.

Sense Perception?

Our senses are appropriate for perceiving material objects such as trees. But "we have no natural faculty for perceiving spiritual beings."[2] We do not (normally) see the angels and the one they worship. God is not demonstrable to sense perception. Thus, we are dependent on revelation and grace if we are indeed to see, and if we are to see God, we must become spiritual. "Very truly, I tell you, no one can enter the kingdom of God without being born of water and Spirit" (John 3:5). We who are God's image are called to return to him who is our archetype. In so doing, we become like angels insofar as we know God not in relation to his effects (created things) but through himself.

God's divinity—his divine nature—is manifest in the things he has made. Created things declare the existence of their Creator. But do they declare the manner of his existence? Here we must proceed with great care. Are we to indeed disregard "sense perception," as Gregory would have us do?[3] Not quite. Rather, sense perception is intrinsic to our becoming spiritual persons. As with the relationship between the literal and the spiritual sense of Scripture, sense perception must yield to spiritual perception. Our senses and our intellect receive their Creator by participation in God's being, invisible, incorporeal, and simple as it is. Our senses and intellect have being and integrity in relation to a principle. That principle is God, Godhead itself, the one essence common to the three persons of the holy and blessed Trinity.

Thomas reminds us that God "is not a participated good."[4] Likewise, God does not participate in something called spirit; rather, "God is spirit" (John 4:24).[5] Similarly, God does not participate in divinity. God is, rather, divinity itself. From this flows a basic epistemological

2. E. L. Mascall, *He Who Is: A Study in Traditional Theism* (London: Longmans, 1943), 15.

3. See further Gregory of Nyssa, *Inscriptions of the Psalms* 1.2.15.

4. Thomas Aquinas, *Summa Theologiae* (hereafter *ST*) I.3.2 (trans. Pegis, 1:28).

5. See *ST* I.3.1, s.c., for Thomas's appeal to John 4:24.

consequence—namely, that God "can be represented only by a multiplicity."[6] As he is without composition, God's "being is identical with its attributes."[7] Such a God cannot be known as he is. We cannot know God as he knows himself, but we can nonetheless know him truly by representing the how of his existence, using a multiplicity of names and attributes.

As we unfold something of the manner of God's existence, we must remember that God is not like us. When we say that God is unmoved, we do not mean that God is static but instead that he is at rest. As Maximus the Confessor says, God does not tend "toward some end," and so he is at rest and tranquil *in se*.[8] In contrast, our sense and intellect are always moved—toward God, we hope. Our senses and intellect once were not. They, along with everything else, were (and are) brought by God "from non-being to being." What is "brought from non-being to being is moved (because it tends toward some end)."[9] Our senses and our intellect err when we forget our cause and end. They can no longer fulfill their God-given function by pointing us to their Creator. We cannot see things as they are. Our senses no longer recognize what is plain to them, and our intellect creates idols. Because of sin, our senses and our intellect resist God.

God's manner of existence compels our senses and intellect to recognize not only their relatedness to God but also God's rationale for blessing us with them in the first place. We were made to "participate proportionally in God."[10] Our intellect and sense perception participate only insofar as they move toward God. When this happens, we "become fit to participate in God."[11] There are epistemological and moral consequences intrinsic to this truth. In terms of the former, we describe God via names that are true of him, though we know not

6. *ST* I.3.3, ad. 2 (trans. Pegis, 1:29).

7. Augustine, *City of God* 11.10, trans. Henry Bettenson (London: Penguin, 2003), 441.

8. Maximus the Confessor, *Ambiguum* 7.1, in *On the Cosmic Mystery of Jesus Christ*, trans. Paul M. Blowers and Robert Louis Wilken (Crestwood, NY: St. Vladimir's Seminary Press, 2003), 46.

9. Maximus the Confessor, *Ambiguum* 7.1.

10. Maximus the Confessor, *Ambiguum* 7.2.

11. Maximus the Confessor, *Ambiguum* 7.2.

how. In terms of the latter, we are to assume ever-greater likeness to God in word and deed.

If God is perfect rest and nothing is predicated of God—goodness is not, for example, predicated of God, for God is goodness itself—our senses and intellect participate in this God "by constant striving toward God."[12] The manner of God's existence may only be described to the extent that we strive. The manner of God's existence—rest, absolute completeness in itself—is known only in movement, striving. This is how we who are corporeal and composite participate in God who "is unmoved and complete and impassible."[13]

Virtue

One might ask whether the language of "participation" displaces prominent New Testament (specifically Pauline) motifs such as justification and sanctification. Does it shortchange the disruptive force of God's justifying and sanctifying work in Christ, with all of its epistemological and moral consequences? In short, no. The virtues are key to understanding why. The virtues contain the "divine form . . . imprinted in them."[14] Now, there are two ways of looking at this. First, the virtues are analogous to what is true of God. God is goodness, love, beauty, and truth. The virtues are creaturely manifestations or likenesses of what is undivided in God. Second, "the substance of virtue in each person" is the Lord Jesus Christ. He declares to us what is, for example, God's righteousness, and it is he who in his Spirit makes righteous. When Maximus writes, "Our Lord Jesus Christ himself is the substance of all the virtues," he cites 1 Corinthians 1:30—"Christ Jesus, who became for us wisdom from God, and righteousness and sanctification and redemption."[15] Righteousness, sanctification, and redemption are virtues, as they are "perfect gift[s]" given by God (James 1:17).

Virtue talk thus has a christological referent. We should want to be virtuous because "every person who participates in virtue as a

12. Maximus the Confessor, *Ambiguum* 7.2.
13. Maximus the Confessor, *Ambiguum* 7.2.
14. Gregory of Nyssa, *Inscriptions of the Psalms* 1.4.30.
15. Maximus the Confessor, *Ambiguum* 7.2.

matter of habit unquestionably participates in God, the substance of the virtues."[16] To be virtuous is to participate in God; to be virtuous is to trust in Christ—to appropriate Paul's confession, "it is no longer I who live, but it is Christ who lives in me" (Gal. 2:20)—and thus be made virtuous in him through the Spirit.

The virtues, which are many, are one in God. In considering the virtues, we gain insight into God's manner of existence. Accordingly, we would not say that God is virtuous but that God is the substance of virtue. Similarly, Jesus is justification, yes, but this is something he became for us on the basis of who he is (God's Son) and what he is (Godhead itself). If we did not take the manner of God's existence seriously, it would be easy for us to say that God is the virtues rather than their substance. It would also be easy to think of them as something outside God in which God participates. And it would be all too easy to think of them in a restrictive sense, as something we pursue in tangential relation to God. But none of that is true. Maximus instead encourages a theocentric understanding. As we increase in virtue, we grow more like God; we become the wisdom, goodness, and righteousness that are ours in Jesus Christ. We become God, "being made God by God."[17]

Note that Maximus talks about virtue in archetypal terms. Virtue is something that we strive to acquire and that God brings about in us. We strive to acquire what is true of God and to live in likeness to God, trusting that what we do is grounded in God and is, more and more, coincident with him. As we increase in virtue, we who are made in God's image return to the likeness of our archetype—God. God's manner of existence is archetypal. God is "the end set for" us.[18] The virtues, coming as they do from God, incline us toward God. Anything in us that is good is of God, who is completely good. God

16. Maximus the Confessor, *Ambiguum* 7.2.

17. Maximus the Confessor, *Ambiguum* 7.2.

18. Maximus makes this point (God's manner of existence as archetypal) in relation to Gregory Nazianzen, *Oration* 28.18, cited in Maximus the Confessor, *Ambiguum* 7.3. Maximus writes, "It is such things, I believe, that this saintly man [Gregory Nazianzen] meant when he said: 'For then we will mingle our god-formed mind and our divine reason with what is properly its own and the image will return to the archetype it now longs for.'" See Maximus the Confessor, *Ambiguum* 7.2, for "the end set for" us.

shares what is his with us who are not God but who by his grace are being renewed in his likeness, Jesus Christ. Simplicity is the principle for soteriology.

Soteriological motifs in the New Testament, such as justification and sanctification, and the motif of divinization, as championed by Maximus and hinted at in 2 Peter 1:4, are complementary. "Thus he has given us, through these things, his precious and very great promises, so that through them you may escape from the corruption that is in the world because of lust, and may become participants of the divine nature" (2 Pet. 1:4). What is true of God in an utterly simple and undivided sense is true of us in Jesus and the Spirit. In Maximus's unforgettable words, the human "becomes wholly God in body and soul by grace and by the unparalleled divine radiance of blessed glory appropriate to him."[19] This maps nicely onto Paul's language in 1 Corinthians 1:30: "He is the source of your life in Christ Jesus, who became for us wisdom from God, and righteousness and sanctification and redemption." We—believers—become in Christ what God is by nature, and we increasingly resemble the manner of God's existence. Maximus calls this a "blessed inversion." The human "is made God by divinization and God is made man by hominization."[20] God's manner of existence is inherently communicative, making divine what is not divine through the process of our becoming truly human. The connection between simplicity and soteriology is therefore straightforward. Fellowship with God is not a manner of our enjoying some "portion of God."[21]

Participation in God is concomitant with desire for God, and that desire for God becomes, as Maximus notes, "more intense and has no limit."[22] We who desire God will never be satiated. God's manner of existence is such that we who remain "wholly [hu]man in soul and body by nature" shall never become "wholly God" in such a way that we cease to be creatures and cease desiring.[23] There will

19. Maximus the Confessor, *Ambiguum* 7.3.
20. Maximus the Confessor, *Ambiguum* 7.2.
21. Gregory Nazianzen, *Oration* 14.7 ("On Love for the Poor"), quoted in Maximus the Confessor, *Ambiguum* 7.2.
22. Maximus the Confessor, *Ambiguum* 7.3.
23. Maximus the Confessor, *Ambiguum* 7.3.

not be anything in us that is not of God. Because God is infinite, we shall never become bored with God or so resemble God that we cease to seek and hunger after him. Accordingly, the manner of God's existence has consequences all the way down, doctrinally speaking, including soteriology's present and future (eschatological) dimensions.

Moses's Example

Gregory cites Psalms 90:1, writing that Moses becomes "the kind of person who no longer needed to be led by law, but could himself become the author of a law for others."[24] Moses is exemplary—hence his being "the author of a law for others." God is intimate with Moses in a way that God is not with others. Moses has experienced terrifying proximity to God, the result being that there is precious little left in Moses that is not of God and commensurate with God. "The LORD used to speak to Moses face to face, as one speaks to a friend" (Exod. 33:11). As Gregory notes, Moses "imitates the deity by beneficence, by doing that which is the distinctive characteristic of the divine nature."[25] The deity whose simple manner of existence is not comprehended by us may nonetheless be imitated by beneficence. The more beneficent we are, the more we are like God and the more we become our true selves—creatures in relation to God.

Consideration of God's manner of existence is fertile ground for Christian devotion, a devotion that Moses exemplifies.[26] Such a life entails doing that which is "characteristic of the divine nature." God "always continues to be what it [i.e., he] is, but the other [i.e., the human] is in the process of becoming what it is not."[27] Because God is fully himself, completely actual, he is the one true means by which we can return to what we once were—beings who live in intimacy

24. Gregory of Nyssa, *Inscriptions of the Psalms* 1.7.50. Note that Psalm 89 for Gregory is Psalm 90 in our modern English translation.
25. Gregory of Nyssa, *Inscriptions of the Psalms* 1.7.57.
26. E. L. Mascall, in his marvelous study, says this of Thomas: "St. Thomas's definition of God is fertile of all the fullness of Catholic devotion." *He Who Is*, 13.
27. Gregory of Nyssa, *Inscriptions of the Psalms* 1.8.77.

with him. Prior to our upending of the Creator-creature relationship, we walked with God in the garden, and by God's grace we are becoming those whom God will permeate in unimaginable intimacy in the life of the world to come. This intimacy will not be the end of us but only the end of everything in us that is not of God. We will exist in God and in likeness to God.

A corollary to God as subsistent being itself is that God is changeless. God's names, whether essential, personal, or proper, are God himself. God is love. God is tripersonal. God cannot change into something that he is not. The perfection we await in heaven, therefore, would be groundless were God not his names and were God not always to be the one he has been. Because God exists simply and in limitless perfection, imitation of him changes us but not God. "The being of the creature must indeed be *analogous* to God's pure act of being."[28] Our goal is God's likeness. Like Moses, we strive to become those who know and will only in relation to what God knows and wills, which is himself, the pure act of being he is. God's grace and our striving to be "analogous" to God are coincident. In Maximus's words, "He remains wholly man in soul and body by nature, and becomes wholly God in body and soul by grace."[29]

The manner of God's existence—his simplicity, that he is without composition—is secondary to God's existence. Following Thomas, God's simplicity is not the first thing to be said, as is the case with God's most proper name, I AM. But simplicity is extremely important nonetheless. It is a correlate, a truth indicative of God's proper name, He Who Is. Simplicity is neither a generic nor a personal name but a term that describes God's manner of existence as fully actual. If the Christian life is about our being "analogous" to God, we are most like God when we live virtuously. This is (again) God's work all the way down. We do not become simple; but in our being divinized, what is true of God in a simple sense becomes true of us in a composite sense. We remain composite. But we are united to God in Christ, desiring him to such an extent that the purity and simplicity of his being so fills us that we become his friends.

28. David Bentley Hart, *The Hidden and the Manifest: Essays in Theology and Metaphysics* (Grand Rapids: Eerdmans, 2017), 99.
29. Maximus the Confessor, *Ambiguum* 7.3.

Familiarity with God

The Father and Son promise to come to us (see John 14:23). Their names—most especially their love—become ours through faith. What is common to them by nature is and will become common to us by grace. Grace, as we said earlier, makes us virtuous. The virtues of God make us virtuous, spiritual. What has primacy from the point of view of theology—God—has primacy from the point of view of devotion. If we are to imitate God, to be conformed to our archetype through faith, hope, and love, then thought of God's manner of existence is profoundly important. Without God we cannot be creatures sharing in the life common to the Three—"human in the fullest sense because divine in the fullest sense."[30]

The Christian life is ultimately about gaining "familiarity with God." Maximus notes, "By practicing the virtues the body gains familiarity with God and becomes a fellow servant with the soul." The locus of the body is that of the soul. The body together with the soul must practice what is commensurate with God. "Through desire and intense love," the Christian "holds fast to God and participates in the divine life." Further, "the result," notes Maximus, is that "the one God, Creator of all, is shown to reside proportionately in all beings through human nature."[31] The language of "proportion" is key. In becoming familiar with God, we are not subsumed into God, erased as it were. No, God resides in us (in increasing measure, it is hoped) in a way proportional to us. This emphasis on virtues, on "familiarity with God," on becoming a certain sort of person "through desire and intense love," need (again) not be opposed to New Testament idioms like justification. We would like to desire and love, indeed practice, the virtues. And yet, following from Romans 7:14–25, we do not. We must "live in love." Jesus tells an unnamed rich young ruler to sell what he has and give to the poor (see Luke 18:18–23 and parallels). He says that many are not worthy of him. "Whoever loves father or mother more than me is not worthy of me; and whoever loves son or daughter more than me is not worthy of me; and whoever does not take up the cross and follow me is not

---

30. Hart, *The Hidden and the Manifest*, 112.
31. Maximus the Confessor, *Ambiguum* 7.4.

worthy of me" (Matt. 10:37–38). A lack of virtue leads to unworthiness before him. God cannot reside in those who are without virtue. Pauline teaching on justification by faith—the faithfulness of Christ—does not contradict the teaching of Maximus. When we practice virtue, we do so in and through the good God who grants us participation in what is "most characteristic of his goodness."[32] The form of that participation is Christ, its basis the life common to the Three.

The work of the soul is to desire and love, the body's work to practice virtue. When the body is given over to virtue, and the soul to desire and love, we receive familiarity with God. Virtue's function, then, is that of restraining the flesh—the anti-God power of which Paul speaks so eloquently in Romans 7:14–25. This is the power that alienates us from God and one another. The virtues that we are to practice in the body and soul are the means by which God resides in us. Neither the body nor the soul is exempt from desire for God to reside. The Creator wills to reside, proportionately, through our nature, which is body and soul, and in ever-increasing degrees.

God, in residing in us, does not annihilate us. Rather, residing is the means by which "independent existence" is given to us. How does God reside? God gives us a particular pedagogical gift, suffering. For example, Paul suffers the inability to do what is good. By acknowledging what he cannot do, the good that is most characteristic of God, Paul departs from "non-being"—sin—and so regains "the capacity to love what is."[33] The inability to do what is good is common to all descendants of Adam's race; thus we confess our inability to gain familiarity with God. Accordingly, we do not run away from Jesus Christ, dejected by the force of his gentle command—"take up the cross and follow me." Instead, we see that in him God has introduced the most marvelous way. This way of Christ is even better than Eden, for it is heaven. There is no possibility of lapsing into what he has defeated and destroyed once and for all.[34]

---

32. Maximus the Confessor, *Ambiguum* 7.4.
33. Maximus the Confessor, *Ambiguum* 7.4.
34. Maximus develops this point with great insight in *Ambiguum* 42 (Excerpt).

What Maximus calls the "gift of deification," which the incarnate Son bestows through the Spirit, is a gift that makes us angel-like.[35] The manner of God's existence—complete purity, ceaseless life—is ours by grace. Like the angels, our mode of existence becomes one of unceasing praise. The corruption that is ours is destroyed, and we are returned to our Maker. The end of the gift of deification is the same as that of justification, sanctification, and redemption. It is one of communion with the Trinity, union with the three persons and all that is common to them not only in terms of their nature but indeed in terms of their manner of existence. The end is friendship, seeing that is face to face. The manner of God's existence determines what we should strive for as Christians—namely, an analogous existence in which there is nothing in us that is not permeated by and transparent to God and to all that he is in his pure act of being. This gift is (again) one for which we must strive. Perfection is rooted in an indicative—what God has done—and contains an imperative: be imitators of the God who has done these things.

Because God truly is, we who are in God by grace will truly be. We will be "in being."[36] This is our hope and the principle of our existence. In the life to come, we will see God and we will see him in all, for he will be all in all, and all will delight in the radiant life of him and the Lamb. Knowledge will have given way to inexpressible delight and vision. All things will be in God in a supreme harmony. All things will declare all that God is, "having become an instrument for God in rhythmical music."[37]

We become instruments of God by God, yes, and we must make ourselves worthy of being such instruments. Deification involves analogous action. God does not need to make himself worthy of anything, whereas we need to make ourselves worthy of God. We do so, Gregory of Nyssa says, by being "zealous about our own life, so that nothing unrhythmical or out of harmony should occur in daily pursuits." Zeal is anchored in prayer. Our life becomes a prayer, one that imitates God, for prayer is imitated "by life."[38] When we pray and

35. Maximus the Confessor, *Ambiguum* 42.
36. Gregory of Nyssa, *Inscriptions of the Psalms* 1.8.106.
37. Gregory of Nyssa, *Inscriptions of the Psalms* 1.9.115.
38. Gregory of Nyssa, *Inscriptions of the Psalms* 2.3.29.

praise, we discover truths of the triune life that would not otherwise be accessible. We discover a horizon unavailable "to what might be discovered about him [God] by human nature."[39] Prayer and praise provide a privileged epistemological window. It is privileged, yes, but it is the privilege afforded by recognition of our own poverty. When we are zealous about our life, when our life becomes prayer, then we know how poor is our manner of life before God in all the fullness of his existence. But again, that poverty is the means by which our prayers are intensified and our manner of existence becomes more akin to God's. As Gregory says, "The intensity of prayer becomes animated and deep-seated when we know in what things we are poor."[40]

The Soul's Elevation in Prayer

It is time to devote attention to the impact of God's simple manner of existence on prayer. We think rightly about these matters by prayer and in prayer. This is the genius of the Psalter. The Psalter provides the best way forward for advancing our thinking in a manner that is confessional, prayer-filled, and praise-filled. How can we appreciate the infinite depth of God's manner of existence unless we live in accordance with virtue? The Psalter's brilliance, notes Gregory, lies in its "design," which makes it easier to live virtuously and to accept "enigmatic teaching of the mysteries."[41] The Psalms encourage us to "taste and see" the goodness of God (Ps. 34:8). Appreciating God's manner of existence, which is "a hard and intense pursuit," to be sure, is not so hard and intense when we sing, lament, and give thanks to God. Even better, when we sing and receive prayer from (and also pray for) others, we "think rightly about these matters."[42] What is so refreshing about Gregory's and Maximus's works, in this regard, is the priority they assign the prayerful life as virtue's form. If we do not pray, we will speak falsely of God. Virtue is the path toward knowing God's manner of existence. If our hearts are not pure, our understanding will not be pure.

39. Gregory of Nyssa, *Inscriptions of the Psalms* 2.3.34.
40. Gregory of Nyssa, *Inscriptions of the Psalms* 2.3.34.
41. Gregory of Nyssa, *Inscriptions of the Psalms* 1.3.17.
42. Maximus the Confessor, *Ambiguum* 7.4.

Another way to say this is that the theologian must be born again.[43] Without being "perpetually born by the Spirit in the exercise of free choice," we are unable to "dignify" the divine oracles, to say nothing of "acquiring the additional gift of assimilation to God by keeping the divine commandment."[44] The theologian encourages the honoring of God's work and assimilation to the God who works. If she is to do so, she herself must revere God, becoming assimilated to him by obedient living.

God is being itself. When we live in relationship with God, we live, as Gregory notes, "in being," which "is truly to be."[45] True creaturely life is imitative. A life of imitation is a life "in being." We imitate God's manner of existence through the "diversity of the virtues." Insofar as we do, we "become an instrument for God in rhythmical music."[46] We become a "spiritual creation," joining with the angels, producing with them "the good sound."[47] Our life accordingly takes on a heavenly hue, given over to pure praise insofar as we live in being itself, which is God.

Here again we have to distinguish between God's manner of existence and our own. God does not engage in praise. There is nothing and no one outside God before whom God must render himself worthy. God does not need improvement, but God does improve us. God does not lack rhythm and harmony, but we do, and so we pray, thereby seeking a life of virtue. God, of course, does not pray for himself, but the Lord Jesus, in and through his Spirit, does pray for us. God never ceases to be, whereas we, when we abscond from God, cease to be. We must pray. Through prayer we remain zealous about our life in such a way that our life becomes a prayer itself. We live "in being." Without prayer we can only proceed so far in our inquiry. We cannot begin to see the invisible God. Accordingly, because God remains "beyond sense-perception and knowledge," we pray.[48] In praying, we acquire knowledge that exceeds our nature. We discover

---

43. Maximus speaks of three births. See *Ambiguum* 42 (Excerpt).
44. Maximus the Confessor, *Ambiguum* 42.
45. Gregory of Nyssa, *Inscriptions of the Psalms* 1.8.103.
46. Gregory of Nyssa, *Inscriptions of the Psalms* 1.8.115.
47. Gregory of Nyssa, *Inscriptions of the Psalms* 1.8.122.
48. Gregory of Nyssa, *Inscriptions of the Psalms* 1.8.110.

things that are superior, far superior, to us. When our life becomes prayer, we sense afresh how poor is our manner of existence in relation to God's. But we also know that in such poverty there is great spiritual wealth. We know that we are poor "in being," that we are not worthy. We must therefore make every effort to become worthy by taking up the cross.

Inasmuch as we strive to become worthy of Christ, we exist in likeness to God—"whoever does not take up the cross and follow me is not worthy of me" (Matt. 10:38). We truly exist insofar as we reflect God's presence and resemble him. To reflect his glory is to image him. Without such imaging, there is little knowledge of God. Unsurprisingly, we image God by praying; in prayer we receive existence afresh, true likeness to God. We become truly human, reflecting the existence of God, who is pure goodness itself. This is our vocation. God's manner of existence determines our vocation. Accordingly, let us love him whose being gives existence to us.

This staggering truth shows us how God's simplicity, his simple manner of existence, will always exceed us, throughout this life and the life of the world to come. Yes, we shall be deified forever, but not in such a way that what is God's by nature will also be ours by nature. We shall never be self-existent. God, however, will always be "all that he *has*" and is.[49] Our union with God—real as it is—is one in which we are always on the receiving end. Our being is accidental. Our existence in the life of the world to come, as with this life, is not self-existence as is God's but always only contingent. We will possess the simplicity that is God's only in a subjective or relative sense. All that we are is of God and God alone, which is the mark of a flourishing creature.

We will never finish with God. A God who is all that he is—such a God is supremely worthy of an eternity of devotion. So great is his glory that the more we become worthy of him by taking up the cross of Christ, the more we sense God's extraordinary grandeur. We shall see, but only as creatures, creatures that are God, yes, but only by participation. Our participation in the God who is at once immanent to us and transcendent of us is explained by the soul's

49. Mascall, *He Who Is*, 117.

elevation into God's self-knowledge. We strive to know God in line
with God's own knowledge of himself. We are known by God if we
share in such knowledge. The profound intimacy of God "in the
soul by grace" is never simply a given, as Eric Mascall notes. It is
nonetheless "offered to anyone who is prepared to live by the theological virtues." It is held forth, indeed, as a gift, one that elevates
and blesses the soul in its quest to love and to be united with God.
We may by grace, through the divine humanity of Jesus Christ, be
united to God. Mascall describes this as "the Spiritual Marriage or
the Prayer of Union."[50]

"Description of the life of the soul in grace" is the telos of an
account of God's names. The doctrine of God is not simply a matter of unfolding but of prescribing "the life of the soul in grace," if
the presentation of God's names be remotely worthy of God. The
doctrine of God "touches," as Mascall notes, "the very nerve of the
Christian life."[51] We are judged by the measure of God, and if the
being described is any less than the great I AM, then we are guilty
of "conceptual idolatry."[52]

Those who see (a Johannine motif) and hear (a synoptic motif)
become less and less capable of experiencing evil. Such people become
angel-like, even as they become Godlike. Their life is, increasingly,
one of praise. Stronger than that, their life is not "merely" one of
praise, but, as Gregory says, they "have no other desire than to prepare their life to be praise of God."[53] Angelic existence is pure praise.
After all, what else could the angels do but praise given that they
"continually see the face of my [Jesus's] Father in heaven" (Matt.
18:10). The angels exist, as does God, insofar as they do not change.
We, however, are "situated with alteration and change on both sides,"
becoming "either worse or better by our alternative activity."[54] We
can and so often do make judgments that are quite wrong and thus
injurious to the soul. But the angels do not. Just as is the case with
God's manner of existence, angelic existence is, on this side of the

50. Mascall, He Who Is, 146.
51. Mascall, He Who Is, 146.
52. Mascall, He Who Is, 197.
53. Gregory of Nyssa, Inscriptions of the Psalms 2.7.71.
54. Gregory of Nyssa, Inscriptions of the Psalms 2.4.39.

angelic rebellion, immovable. They "continually see," and so are held in endless praise of the one they see. At the same time, the angels, as with those among us who are being made better, do not exist as does God, who is divine by nature.

Ascetical Existence

One of the imperatival consequences of God's manner of existence is that we must change if we are to be like him who is without change. The only way we "acquire that change to what is superior" is, Gregory notes, "by means of prayer and diligence of life."[55] The most fitting response to God's manner of existence is prayer. The change that "prayer and diligence of life" reap is, in part, righteousness. "The hidden things of the knowledge of God, the source of which is faith in the Son," become less hidden, more manifest.[56] Knowledge of these hidden things is acquired through cleansing, and what cleanses is "the assault of the trials."[57]

God does not need to be cleansed. As one who is pure spirit, immaterial and absolutely good, there is no potential in him whereby he could do evil. But we are not God, and we do not yet have a place in the angelic chorus. We are creatures that must learn to abscond from evil. By virtue of our flesh, that anti-God power, we operate "by means of perceptible things" and so are oblivious to spiritual things. However, when we pray and exercise "diligence of life," we encourage "spiritual and immaterial life . . . in the intellectual and incorporeal life of the soul."[58] Thomas speaks insightfully of this, calling prayer "the interpreter of desire."[59] Though it would appear that the souls of the saints are outwardly wasting away, they are being renewed day by day. That renewal is a fruit of God's life. As with the tabernacle of old, God desires to indwell us, abide in and among his people, writing his law on our hearts.

55. Gregory of Nyssa, *Inscriptions of the Psalms* 2.4.48.
56. Gregory of Nyssa, *Inscriptions of the Psalms* 2.5.49.
57. Gregory of Nyssa, *Inscriptions of the Psalms* 2.6.61.
58. Gregory of Nyssa, *Inscriptions of the Psalms* 2.6.64.
59. See, e.g., *ST* II-II.83.1, ad. 1, quoted in Paul Murray, OP, *Praying with Confidence: Aquinas on the Lord's Prayer* (London: Continuum, 2010), 37n23.

The more diligent we are in prayer, the more our existence comes to resemble God's. We separate from evil, "coming to be in the good, and becoming like God so far as possible."[60] We become like God by becoming better, seeking thereby our being in the one who knows neither increase nor improvement, "whose being always exists since he has not come into being from anything."[61] We truly enjoy our creatureliness, for we receive it in relation to God. In desiring God we become creatures whose lives are conformed to Christ. Christ's form is our form, for there becomes nothing in us that is not of him. We feed on him eucharistically, becoming what he is, divine, for there is nothing that is his that he has not communicated to us in his Spirit. In Jesus Christ, we become like God, consumed by God's life but not destroyed. Jesus Christ is our advocate and mediator. Even when we reach perfection, and the Father is "all in all," the Father will continue to communicate his life to us, the life that we have always received from him through Christ in the Spirit (1 Cor. 15:28).

God shares with us not just what he is but also the way in which he is. The manner of God's existence, as one who is all that he is, is communicable. God shares his eternal life with us in Jesus and the Spirit. We are re-created in Christ as those fit for God. Our manner of existence is capable of becoming divine through his indwelling of us. God, all that he is, is ours, in and through Jesus Christ by the power of the Spirit, received in Word and sacrament. Jesus gives what is his, all that is proper to him and the Father and the Spirit, and takes upon himself, in a way that draws to mind Luther's teaching on the great exchange, what is ours.[62] Like the burning bush, we are consumed but not destroyed. Nothing that we are is part of God: God does not exist as we do. And this we know only insofar as we worship and obey. We join with Job in dust and ashes, declaring the Lord to be "too wonderful" for us (Job 42:3).

60. Gregory of Nyssa, *Inscriptions of the Psalms* 2.8.73.
61. Gregory of Nyssa, *Inscriptions of the Psalms* 2.8.80.
62. Luther writes, "Christ is full of grace, life, and salvation. The soul is full of sins, death, and damnation. Now let faith come between them and sin, death, and damnation will be Christ's, while grace, life, and salvation will be the soul's." Luther, "The Freedom of a Christian," in *Martin Luther's Basic Theological Writings*, ed. Timothy F. Lull (Minneapolis: Fortress, 1989), 603.

God's way of being God, his simple manner of existence, is, as I have been arguing, fruitful for understanding Christian life on ascetical terms. Christian life is an ascetical life. When we live ascetically—indeed, virtuously—the Spirit forms "our souls in accordance with God through virtue."[63] The active agent in this is of course the Spirit, who does what we cannot do—namely, conform us to God via imitation of him. The tool that the Spirit uses is Scripture. The aim of this tool—especially the Psalms—is "the divine likeness."[64] The more we are like him, the more human we are, and the more human we are, the more we resemble him as his likeness. We grow in being, becoming more rather than less real, and all that because we live in a believing relation to the one who "is being."[65] We thereby flee corruption. We resist the sinful tendency to remove ourselves from being. Nothing could be worse than to be without God. Thus, we must believe and in faith encourage virtue.

In all of this, we keep coming back to Scripture, spiritually received. We read "the inspired words to perceive the spiritual sense in them."[66] Scripture prepares us, in this life, for praise of God's glory, and sight of the glorious God in the next. We require a spiritual sense. Perception and reception of the spiritual sense, however, requires "great nobility" of heart.[67] Nobility of heart is how we go about understanding what cannot be contained but can, nonetheless, be participated in. In mortifying the flesh, in learning to desire none but God, we become spiritual, feeding our spirits with the inspired Word.

We will suffer ill, as Gregory notes, but the blessing of that suffering is participation. The suffering that is attendant on faith does not simply privilege the sufferer in an epistemological sense. Even more, suffering ill because of "labours for virtue" grants participation, a share in the divine likeness, which nothing could be better than.[68] God is our best thought by day and by night: may there be less and less in

63. Gregory of Nyssa, *Inscriptions of the Psalms* 2.11.135.
64. Gregory of Nyssa, *Inscriptions of the Psalms* 2.11.137.
65. Gregory of Nyssa, *Inscriptions of the Psalms* 2.13.186.
66. Gregory of Nyssa, *Inscriptions of the Psalms* 2.14.231.
67. Gregory of Nyssa, *Inscriptions of the Psalms* 2.14.240.
68. Gregory of Nyssa, *Inscriptions of the Psalms* 2.15.260.

us that is not of him, less and less in us that does not bear witness to what he is and how he exists.

"The Moral Race Course" of the Baptized

Christian life, the life of the new birth as it were, is from God, and its form is cruciform. Baptism structures our imitation of God. Let me explain. We are reborn by God in order to seek likeness to God in accordance with the image of God, Jesus Christ. "The manner of birth from God," Maximus notes, not only bestows "the grace of adoption" but also "introduces, wholly by active exertion, that grace which deliberately reorients the entire free choice of the one being born of God toward the God who gives birth."[69] Maximus does not oppose divine agency—the new birth is of God—to active exertion, and neither should we. To be born of God is to wholly lean toward God. The second dimension of the new birth takes us beyond faith to knowledge. It is "active exertion" that "engenders in the knower the sublimely divine likeness of the One known."[70] New birth is birth unto likeness, likeness of the one not only believed in but also known. In reorienting ourselves toward God, we acquire true knowledge of God, true because "acquired by exertion."[71] Such knowledge "transfigures the mind with the blessed light-rays of our God and Father."[72]

Herein we see the prescriptive power of teaching on God. Intrinsic to Maximus's reworking of the Johannine command to new birth is a subtle account not only of the relationship between the literal and spiritual senses of Scripture but also of the shape of the spiritual life. The literal meaning encourages the spiritual. However, the literal meaning is unleashed in the Spirit and is available only to those "with spiritual eyes."[73] "Spiritual eyes," indeed "the eyes of the

---

69. Maximus the Confessor, *Quaestiones ad Thalassium* 6 ("On the Grace of Holy Baptism").

70. Maximus the Confessor, *Quaestiones ad Thalassium* 6.

71. Maximus the Confessor, *Quaestiones ad Thalassium* 6.

72. Maximus the Confessor, *Quaestiones ad Thalassium* 6.

73. Maximus the Confessor, *Quaestiones ad Thalassium* 17 ("On Spiritual Progress in Virtue").

soul," discern the "saving meaning" in the literal. When Scripture is received this way, it is truly "good and noble." But again, to receive it with "the eyes of the soul," we are required to enter on a spiritual marathon of sorts. The passions that arise in us must be rendered pure in the context of what Maximus calls, evocatively, "the moral race course of life."[74]

Racing on this course, however, is dependent on baptismal grace from beginning to end. Its foundation is "the mystery of the divine incarnation," its intention "the grace of human deification."[75] Our ascent via this racecourse is thus active (not passive), but that action is at all times a work of grace. One day, however, our activity—as we know it, anyhow—shall cease. We shall worshipfully rest in the repose of God's pure actuality, present in all things in the life of the world to come. We will cease to strive, God infinitely deifying those who are open to him. The life of the world to come will be marked on our part by "a spiritual faculty, unlimited in potential, . . . capable of transcending the nature of all created beings and known things."[76] The eschatological horizon completes, then, an account of God's manner of existence understood with respect to its impact on us. We shall not one day leave behind our creatureliness, and we shall not one day reach a deified state. Rather, we "will [one day] unwittingly enter into the true Cause of existent being and terminate our proper faculties."[77] The Lord will lift us above our "proper limits." And yet, until then, we must exercise even as our deification, which enables "God to become incarnate" within us, takes place "by grace." Our "transformation unto deification" rests on God's goodness toward us. His goodness never ceases.[78] We will always receive from him, not he from us.

The burden of this book, so far, has been to expand our sense of the relevance of God's existence, his simple manner of existence, to the Christian life. I have encouraged knowing as a fruit of ascetical

74. Maximus the Confessor, *Quaestiones ad Thalassium* 17.
75. Maximus the Confessor, *Quaestiones ad Thalassium* 22 ("On Jesus Christ and the End of the Ages").
76. Maximus the Confessor, *Quaestiones ad Thalassium* 22.
77. Maximus the Confessor, *Quaestiones ad Thalassium* 22.
78. Maximus the Confessor, *Quaestiones ad Thalassium* 22.

experience. Experience of divine things renders us, I think, worthy of divinity itself. Ascetical knowledge is the highest form of knowing available to us in this life. Maximus describes this dynamic in quite a magnificent way. He writes, "The scriptural Word knows of two kinds of knowledge of divine things." There is what he calls "relative knowledge," which is knowledge "rooted only in reason and ideas, and lacking in the kind of experiential perception of what one knows through active engagement." Relative knowledge—staid, cerebral, and placid—is quite the opposite of "truly authentic knowledge," which is "gained only by actual experience, apart from reason and ideas." Knowledge gained by experience "provides a total perception of the known object through a participation by grace." This "total perception" is provided by knowledge of God acquired in the throes of actual experience of God, and yields to participation in the same "by grace."[79]

Importantly, Maximus does not denigrate "relative knowledge based on reason and ideas" but does recognize its limits. Relative knowledge is preparatory, you might say, for the kind of knowledge that truly has the Trinity at its center. Relative knowledge creates a hunger for the kind of knowledge that is greater—namely, "participatory knowledge." Such knowledge takes seriously the command of Christ to "go and do likewise" (Luke 10:37). Just so, "participatory knowledge [is] acquired by active engagement."[80] Participatory knowledge derives from the Psalter, making it such rich ground. The Lord is loved as he is praised, revered as the one who alone can deliver us from our enemies and who delights in rescuing the downtrodden.

Maximus is not encouraging his hearers to become theologians of glory, to storm the heavens as it were. No, his point is that God can be directly perceived, directly known as God, only when God is experienced "by participation." Active knowledge of God is but the fruit of seeking God. "But it is for you, O LORD, that I wait" (Ps. 38:15). If this is correct, those whose lives are exemplary know God with a kind of directness that cannot be said of those whose lives are

79. Maximus the Confessor, *Quaestiones ad Thalassium* 60.
80. Maximus the Confessor, *Quaestiones ad Thalassium* 60.

disordered. The vista afforded by participative knowledge is inaccessible to relative knowledge. Participative knowledge experiences what is supernatural. Think about Elijah and Elisha: they see. Fascinatingly, experience understood as "knowledge, based on active engagement, ... surpasses all reason."[81] Being actively engaged by God's simple manner of existence, by him being all that he is, generates knowledge that transcends reason. But again, such knowledge and experience assume active engagement, a heart that rejoices in the Lord God, a heart that sees.

If we follow Maximus on these points as we consider God's manner of existence as a fruitful rubric for Christian life, we learn that God, in all his incomprehensibility, becomes more precious to us the more we become righteous. Without the righteousness we receive when we yield to Christ, God is nothing to us. Without suffering, we seek other ways of being that do not have God as their center. We construct our own racecourse. We thereby depart from "the only sure foundation of well-being, which is in God."[82]

Our reconciliation in Jesus Christ deifies. Our manner of existence, then, is declared to be like God's, without sin, and it increasingly becomes, in the Spirit, like God's, without sin. We see in the strongest possible terms the imperative at the heart of contemplation of God. If our nature is not in the process of renewal, then that of which we speak is not God.

If such is the case, then, there arises a fresh appreciation of the power of baptismal grace in rendering us like God in "the moral race course." The Spirit in and with which we are sealed in our baptism works without rest to render us open to God. Christ commands certain habits and through the grace of the Spirit brings them about. "Go and do likewise." Only in the life of obedience do we receive glimpses of what God is and God's manner of being God. It is the "setting" for receiving the truth of what and who God is. In embarking on a pilgrimage made possible by what God has done, one hears in faith day in and day out: "I am the LORD your God, who brought you out of the land of Egypt" (Exod. 20:2).

81. Maximus the Confessor, *Quaestiones ad Thalassium* 61 ("On the Legacy of Adam's Transgression").
82. Maximus the Confessor, *Quaestiones ad Thalassium* 61.

But what about Paul in Romans 7:15—"For I do not do what I want, but I do the very thing I hate"? And what about Israel's history of apostasy? Do we not simply refuse to do what we are supposed to do? More strongly put, are we not incapable of and thoroughly indifferent to what we are supposed to do? Yes, our only hope is Christ, who by his Spirit unites us in Word and sacrament to himself and to his body, the church. Accordingly, when we seek God and pray, we, through his grace, receive the new birth, becoming thereby more ordered. We begin to see how absurd is the denial of God's existence. Moral discernment, not disorder, is intrinsic to profession of God's manner of existence. Description of God's existence and his manner of existence is a function of the soul's fulfillment of its vocation: be holy, be reconciled to God. The God who is love is not seen without love. Spiritual progress is not simply a fruit of doctrinal understanding but in many respects a prerequisite and ongoing presupposition. The doctrine of God has an end—namely, the stretching out of our souls "into the infinity of God's goodness, an external pilgrimage into ever-greater depths of divine glory."[83]

The radical interruption of our idolatries by God in Jesus Christ is radically regenerative: new creation is its fruit. I was blind but now I see. But what do I see but the one who has been there all along, declaring "himself in all of being"?[84] We receive spiritual sight and make spiritual progress by praying and rendering praise. Because God is the pure act of being itself, always all that he is in simplicity, he is never catchable as it were. And yet the interruptive heart of teaching on God—that God is not a creature—must not be allowed to displace or be seen as inimical to "the sacramental reality of a fallen world that grows in anticipation of its transformation into the kingdom."[85] The ever-greater dissimilarity between God and us does not encourage any partition between nature and grace.[86] The doctrine of God's ongoing principles is, yes, a graced life—a life of "spiritual progress, bodily inanition, and prayer."[87] Insofar as we live in and imitate God

83. Hart, *The Hidden and the Manifest*, 300.
84. Hart, *The Hidden and the Manifest*, 316.
85. Hart, *The Hidden and the Manifest*, 313.
86. See further Hart, *The Hidden and the Manifest*, 325.
87. Hart, *The Hidden and the Manifest*, 295.

in this moral racecourse, there is less and less in us that is not of him. Our life is made over into a theophany—again, disclosive of nothing that is not of and participant in God.

Conclusion

Though God cannot be seen in this life—God is spirit—we must submit ourselves to a spiritual pedagogy. We shed our "ingrained proclivities toward material objects which keep the mind from being freed from the darkness of ignorance to behold the light of true knowledge."[88] Contemplation of the manner of God's existence gives form to this pedagogy. Because God is immaterial—as pure Spirit—we must become spiritual through the Spirit who shapes us in accordance with the Lord, the life-giving Spirit. We only then grow discontent with understanding what is made through our self-enclosed existence. We cannot free ourselves to love what is unmade. We may say, like the people of God on the eve of Joshua's death, "No, we will serve the LORD!" (Josh. 24:21). Even as we say that, however, we know that we have yet to put away our "foreign gods" (Josh. 24:23). Truth be told, we cannot. It is the Lord who liberates us from our bondage, endowing us "with the inextinguishable light of true knowledge and the indefatigable power of the virtues."[89] God is the cause of virtue, the virtue in which we act so as to become spiritual, resembling God as God. God causes godly knowledge by causing virtue. That is my point. The God who causes us wills to transform and perfect us. Though God is spirit and he calls us to be spiritual, his call does not violate our materiality. As Maximus makes clear, grace "transforms nature, without violating it, unto deification."[90]

The parallel is the resurrection body. It is a body, to be sure, but a transformed one. The transformed body is a spiritual body. To imitate God's manner of existence is to become spiritual. This is the absolute antithesis of arrogance and vainglory. When we love what God is and what is convertible with God—goodness and love, for example—then

---

88. Maximus the Confessor, *Quaestiones ad Thalassium* 64 ("On the Prophet Jonah and the Economy of Salvation").
89. Maximus the Confessor, *Quaestiones ad Thalassium* 64.
90. Maximus the Confessor, *Quaestiones ad Thalassium* 64.

we cease to love "anything non-existent."[91] What exists in relation to God—what is in us that is of him—is not only "so much better and more honourable than any existent thing precious to man," but also that for which there is nothing better. It is impossible to talk about God's manner of existence in detached terms. How can we speak of God's simplicity as pure spirit without also voicing that there is nothing better, nothing dearer, than such a God? Nonexistence is what God does not know; it is not dear to God. What exists in and of itself is God, and God supremely delights in himself. What is dear to God ought therefore to be dear to us in relation to God.

In this chapter I have demonstrated how God's manner of existence is exemplary for Christian life. The Christian's manner of existence is to imitate God's manner of existence. There is nothing in God that is not himself. May it increasingly be said of us that there is nothing in us that is not of God.

Love does not reside in God; God *is* love. The Christian is one in whom God sees himself. The lover of God is one whom God knows. Drawing on Gregory and Maximus, with some help from others, we have seen how the manner of God's existence shapes our own. May our lives here and now be a foretaste of what shall ever be, God being "all in all" (1 Cor. 15:28). When our manner of existence resembles God's, our identity is defined not by us as creatures but by God the Creator. What is recognized in us is God. There is nothing more excellent than that.

---

91. Maximus the Confessor, *Quaestiones ad Thalassium* 64.

3

Perfection and the Christian Life

Be perfect, therefore, as your heavenly Father is perfect.

—Matthew 5:48

God's perfection is exemplary for the Christian life. His perfection, as with his existence and simple manner of existence, is archetypal. God's names are the basis for Christian existence. Even more, they may be imitated. "Be imitators of God" (Eph. 5:1). We become like God by imitating God, living a life of love, thereby sharing the divine nature. Christian thinking on God has a home. It starts with faith and is perfected in love. Christian teaching on God is a series of footnotes offered by the pilgrim on her journey toward the promised heavenly land.

To speak of God in ways that are not false requires that we become certain sorts of persons. A program for spiritual progress, for growth toward the Lord God, may be derived from God's way of being God. As Gregory notes, "It is necessary to show through our life that we ourselves are what the power of this name requires us to be."[1] In this

---

1. Gregory of Nyssa, *On Perfection*, in *Ascetical Works*, trans. Virginia Woods Callahan, ed. Roy Joseph Deferrari, Fathers of the Church (Washington, DC: Catholic University of America Press, 1967), 95.

chapter I continue to feel my way forward, describing perfection as a name expressive of a dominical command.[2]

Accordingly, this chapter (as with this book) advances a basic motif. I write with a view toward what our lives must show on the basis of who God recalls himself to be. I assume that what Christian life is to show is what the names require us to show. The divine names are the subject of Christian life and the agent of that life. God perfects those whom he commands to be perfect. I unfold in the pages ahead how impossible it is to speak truthfully and lovingly of the perfect God without our lives imitating and sharing in the divine nature. The Trinity is infinitely more, infinitely better, far greater than we can ever conceive or imagine. Hearing the dominical command to perfection in the Sermon on the Mount in Matthew 5:48 furnishes us with a wonderful opportunity to consider God's perfection and the imperative commensurate with it.

Perfection is true of the one and simple God. God lacks nothing and so is perfect. The Lord exists without reference to anything else, and his manner of existence is as one who is entirely complete. God is all that he is. These things we must say, but how? These truths will never be attested rightly if we are not certain sorts of persons, or on our way to becoming certain sorts of persons. Learning about God's manner of being involves our sharing in what God is through imitation.

If such is the case, doctrine is more than a description of things believed. It presents a form of life, a life toward which we must tend. We are called to (truly) exist, and to exist in a manner that resembles God. "Be perfect." Though absolute perfection is not available to us, what Thomas rather helpfully calls a "middle perfection" is. He writes, "The more one extracts himself from the acts of the world, the more he may think of God actually [*cogitat de Deo in actu*]."[3]

2. See further Augustine, *The Trinity*, trans. Edmund Hill, OP (Brooklyn, NY: New City Press, 1991), 203n20, wherein Hill writes of Augustine's account of what distinguishes the divine persons, "Confusions are part and parcel of Augustine's *via inventionis*, which is so different from Aquinas' *via doctrinae*."

3. Thomas Aquinas, *Commentary on Matthew* 5.12.557, commenting on Matt. 5:48, trans. Jeremy Holmes and Beth Mortensen, available at https://aquinas.cc/la/en/~Matt.

To think of God actually involves imitation, "likeness by imitation."[4] Imitation of God involves death to the ways of the world. The doctrine of God is immensely shortchanged if it gives the impression that you can simply describe the names without attending to their moral, spiritual, and ethical import. As Paul says, "And I live no longer, but the Anointed lives within me" (Gal. 2:20 DBH). We speak of God in faith as those tethered to the Scriptures and immersed in the sacramental life of Christ's body. To the extent that we do so, our relation to God has its appropriate form.

The impulse for this pursuit comes with a growing sense of dissatisfaction with how the doctrine of God has been treated, at least in Protestant modernity. Pursuing the doctrine of God *"under the conditions of modernity,"* as Bruce McCormack says of Karl Barth, means that epistemic concerns often dominate.[5] Knowledge of God is of course important. But Scripture and the premodern tradition remind us that Christian life is the setting for the doctrine of God. You unfold God's names as you become perfect. Divine names are instructive and formative. Imitation, you might say, indicates a different way of knowing, that which we seek, however haltingly, to speak of in faith. Only insofar as we imitate Christ, as did Paul, by becoming perfect as his Father, our Father, is perfect do we "think of God actually." Put boldly, I consider it very difficult to accurately describe God's life without tending toward the same. Imitation, as well as the reverence and worship it gives rise to, is not an afterthought. Indeed, as Gregory notes, one treats God by setting out "an accurate description of the life towards which one must tend."[6]

I will articulate my account of God's perfection based largely on Gregory's treatise *On Perfection*. Furthermore, I will treat existence as including God's simplicity and, as we shall see, his infinity and immutability. The "good qualities connected with Christ" are true of the Father and the Spirit, and in and through our baptism in Christ they are true, too, of us.[7] These "good qualities" are communicated

---

4. Aquinas, *Commentary on Matthew* 5.12.553, commenting on Matt. 5:48.

5. Bruce L. McCormack, *Orthodox and Modern: Studies in the Theology of Karl Barth* (Grand Rapids: Baker Academic, 2008), 232.

6. Gregory of Nyssa, *On Perfection*, 95.

7. Gregory of Nyssa, *On Perfection*, 99.

to us in Christ, and we must grow into them. In Christ and by the Spirit, we are declared perfect before the Father. God's essential names are communicated, to be sure, but that communication is not purely extrinsic. Let me explain.

The Likeness of God

Human beings, like all created beings, "are like God as the first and universal principle of all being." The "like" here must be carefully unfolded. It is analogical in nature. "Being itself is common to all."[8] It is true to say that we—as with the birds of the air—have being. It is not false, moreover, to speak of being in relation to God. However, there is profound dissimilarity between God and us because God is uncreated being, absolute being itself, whereas we have our being by participation.

God creates us for himself; we are compatible with him. Just so, a name like existence is common to God and human beings. God exists and we exist, though not of course in the same way. Existence is not something in which God participates. God exists in relation to himself. This is not true of us, who exist only in relation to him. Our nature does not approximate the simple manner of God's existence. We are composite beings. We can only revere and worship one who is all that he is.

In contrast to existence itself, God's manner of existence, his simplicity, does not apply to our existence in an analogical way common to all. In this life we are not simple like God is. And yet, when we look to the life of the world to come, we see how divine simplicity is realized in us in heaven. To put it in a Thomistic idiom, our life will be convertible with God's, though the reverse will not be true. God will always have life *in se*. In this life, insofar as we love God, there is less and less in us that is not compatible with him. The point, then, is that with the name perfection, as with God's existence, his manner of existence, and, as we shall see, his infinity and immutability, we leave behind analogical discourse. Insofar as we obey the dominical "precept" to perfection, we are more rather than less "like" God.[9] The

---

8. Thomas Aquinas, *Summa Theologiae* (hereafter *ST*) I.4.3 (trans. Pegis, 1:41).
9. Aquinas, *Commentary on Matthew* 5.12.553, commenting on 5:48.

dissimilarity between God and us is increasingly less, not more. In being perfect, we become like God. Perfection has a biblical density that none of our other names have. Jesus does not command us to exist, but he does command us to be perfect. We are created good, indeed very good, but called in Christ to be perfect. God (the Father) is our perfection, and Christian faith is an imitation of the same.

Gregory puts this in an unforgettable way: "If one can give a definition of Christianity, we shall define it as follows: Christianity is an imitation of the divine nature."[10] Christian faith does not simply benefit from talk about imitation of God; the pursuit of God, and of saying things that are true of God, assumes imitation. We can neither consider nor contemplate the goods of the Father if we are not among "those born through him [who are] to be the same in the perfection of the goods contemplated in the Father."[11] Insofar as our hearts and minds are reborn, we are able to share in what is his, including his perfection. Jesus's statement "Blessed are the pure in heart" (Matt. 5:8), Paul's laboring so as to "present every human being as perfected in the Anointed" (Col. 1:28 DBH), and the psalmist's desire to "be blameless in your statutes, so that I may not be put to shame" (Ps. 119:80) indicate in no uncertain terms the urgency of the imperative intrinsic to God's names.

Here we are far beyond a simple description. What we say of God is as important as how we say it. As Anna Williams notes, "Our understanding of who God is cannot be separated from our understanding of how we go about understanding God."[12] We declare the glories of the gospel and its God by virtue of our union with him in faith. We go about understanding God by declaring his glory. "It is entirely necessary for us to become what is contemplated," notes Gregory, "in connection with that incorruptible nature."[13] We are to become what we seek. The descriptive dimension of Christian teaching—the unfolding of what we behold—is important. However,

10. Gregory of Nyssa, *On What It Means to Call Oneself a Christian*, in *Ascetical Works*, trans. Virginia Woods Callahan, ed. Roy Joseph Deferrari, Fathers of the Church (Washington, DC: Catholic University of America Press, 1967), 85.

11. Gregory of Nyssa, *Call Oneself a Christian*, 86.

12. A. N. Williams, *The Architecture of Theology: Structure, System, and Ratio* (Oxford: Oxford University Press, 2011), 135.

13. Gregory of Nyssa, *Call Oneself a Christian*, 86.

it is inadequate by itself. I do not think we ought to describe the contours of the divine life without such giving rise to pedagogy for intimacy with the life of God. In imitation we see the purity of the divine nature. "Be holy, for I am holy" (Lev. 11:44). The word "be," the imperative, precedes the indicative, the words "I am." Of course, there would be no summons to be holy were it not for the holy God. But talk of God's essential holiness, purity, and perfection rests on this call. Again, the order here matters. The Lord does not say, "The Father is perfect, so be perfect." Rather, the fact that the precept precedes the "I am" reminds us of a simple truth: the narrative sequence. Every exhortation assumes the "I AM." The way to consider the "I AM" is by honoring this basic scriptural pattern.

The perfect God encompasses us. Though we do not like to know this, given that we are so often content with being our own gods, the dominical command to be perfect naturalizes us. The more perfect we are, the more human. Why is that? Because we are made for intimacy with our Creator. We are spoken into being so as to look at the birds, hearing the sermons they preach simply by being—"look at the birds of the air" (Matt. 6:26).

The Father is perfect (as are the Son and the Spirit) because there is never any disjunction between his being and his existence. The same is not true of us. In terms of humanity, there is an enormous disjunction between our being and the manner of our existence. "There is no one who is righteous, not even one," writes Paul in Romans 3:10, paraphrasing Ecclesiastes 7:20. We are deemed very good at our creation but rarely do what is very good. In God, however, there is no gap. God's existence is his essence. Jesus's command to be perfect restores us to ourselves, before God. To know God aright is to know ourselves; to be ourselves is to be before God.[14] Perfection is thus attainable in this life. We can "separate ourselves from earthly passions" in this life.[15] Insofar as we do, we become, as Thomas notes, effects who "in some way resemble the form of the agent."[16] Describing

14. See further John Calvin, *Institutes of the Christian Religion*, trans. Ford Lewis Battles, vol. 1 (Philadelphia: Westminster, 1960), 1.1.2: "Without knowledge of God there is no knowledge of self."

15. Gregory of Nyssa, *Call Oneself a Christian*, 88.

16. *ST* I.4.3 (trans. Pegis, 40).

God's names is an "effort in behalf of piety," a matter of becoming and resembling what is contemplated.[17]

Is Christ Perfect?

This raises the question of whether Christ is perfect. Why does Jesus not preach, "Be perfect as I am perfect"? Why is the reference to the Father? Paul and John help us think clearly about this. When Jesus says the Father is "greater," he speaks with reference to his mission. Jesus is sent, the Father sends—hence the Father who sends is "greater" than the one sent (John 14:28). What about Paul? The Lord Jesus, Paul notes, comes "in the likeness of sinful flesh" (Rom. 8:3). The Father is greater insofar as it is the Son, not the Father, who became incarnate. The Son makes himself nothing, appearing as one of us. The Father's "form"—if I may use that word—is "more perfect" than that of the incarnate Son simply because the Son unites himself to "the likeness of sinful flesh." It is the Son, not the Father, who makes himself nothing.

Another way to make this point is in reference to Christ's suffering and the obedience he learns through it (see Heb. 5:8). The suffering of Christ does not affect his identity. The Lord Jesus becomes neither more nor less the Son of God because of his undergoing suffering and death. Even in death he is the Father's eternally begotten and beloved Son. His humanity includes our own, sanctifying it through fidelity to his Father's will.

Jesus sees the Father, and the Father sees him. The Father is rich in every way, not lacking in anything. The Father is perfect and without lack—again, absolute identity with respect to being and existence. On the one hand, the same is true of Jesus: he enacts who he is, God's Son. On the other hand, the Son exists as the one he has always been in a life undergoing death. The flesh he assumes is not naturally divine—he divinizes it. The Lord Jesus is perfect. His mission, which culminates in his becoming sin, discloses his perfection in the "folly" of the cross (1 Cor. 1:18 DBH).

17. Gregory of Nyssa, *On the Christian Mode of Life*, in *Ascetical Works*, trans. Virginia Woods Callahan, ed. Roy Joseph Deferrari, Fathers of the Church (Washington, DC: Catholic University of America Press, 1967), 131.

Perfection thus involves taking on the way of Christ through imitation. As Gregory notes, "It is necessary for anyone desiring to be closely united with another to take on the ways of that person through imitation. Therefore, it is necessary for the one longing to be the bride of Christ to be like Christ in beauty through virtue as far as possible."[18]

The perfect life is something of a contest wherein we seek to be like Christ. The form of that seeking is virtue. Gregory describes virtue as a form of "wealth which God ordained for those who love the contest of love for Christ." The perfect life, indeed the "perfect Christian," is the lover of Jesus Christ.[19] This is someone who hates sin and therefore loves virtue. Virtue, as we have noted, is fairly elastic language. Virtue includes everything from obedience to simplicity of life, including one's commitment to prayer. Christian perfection as a form of virtue is something toward which we must strive. It involves toil. We strive to be virtuous and so to be worthy of Jesus Christ. We must render ourselves worthy of Jesus Christ and the Father, recognizing all the while that it is Jesus who through his Spirit makes us worthy of him. The more we strive to establish ourselves in him, the more we enjoy and see his establishment of us in him. The more we toil and labor, and strive toward perfection, the more are we rooted in Christ's faith, hope, and love. "An unmeasured love of God" is "the foundation of faith."[20] Such love is the way of holy teaching. When we love God, we are not far from the kingdom.

Love is doctrine's ground, its wellspring. We may "understand all mysteries and all knowledge." We may even "have all faith." It is indeed possible to receive God's self-revelation in Christ with understanding, knowledge, and faith "so as to move mountains," but all the while not having love (1 Cor. 13:2). Understanding, knowledge, and faith—the foundation of these is love. The love of God encounters us as we seek perfection, and in pursuing love we obey the commandment. "Love of God," says Gregory, "does not come to us simply or automatically." Jesus's intensification of the law of Moses—"if your right hand causes you to falter, cut it off and fling it away from you"

18. Gregory of Nyssa, *Christian Mode of Life*, 133.
19. Gregory of Nyssa, *Christian Mode of Life*, 143.
20. Gregory of Nyssa, *Christian Mode of Life*, 145.

(Matt. 5:30 DBH)—furnishes the background for the command "Be perfect." Love of God comes "through many sufferings and great concern in cooperation with Christ."[21] Herein we see the kinds of spiritual demands that the perfection of God involves.

Thinking on God that is enamored of heavenly treasure takes its final form in prayer. Prayer is the principal fruit of love for God. Prayer undertaken in secret before the "Father who sees in secret"—there is nothing more annihilating of thoughts not worthy of the perfect God (Matt. 6:4). Without prayer, we are tempted to think of our Father as needing us, as someone enriched by us.

Prayer denotes "inexpressible devotion" to the one who does not need us in order to be.[22] Prayer is not simply the fruit of love but the means by which love is further kindled. Prayer is the crucible that determines what we say about God and how we say it. Prayer is love's triumph. That is why contemplation of God and God's manner of existence assumes its highest form in prayer. We make inquiry about God in order that we may love God, and all that with a view toward praying to and praising him. Consideration of God's existence and manner of existence does not simply inflame a love of the Lord but also serves that same love. The perfection of God ought to be unfolded in such a way as to kindle the desire to be perfect.

Rewards

All Christians are to be perfect, to live, in Gregory's unforgettable words, "the God-loving life."[23] The God-loving life is a life that brings great heavenly rewards, sometimes anticipated even in rewards in this life. Prayer is the means by which we nurture heavenly treasure. Meditation on God and his works and a cheerful embrace of his commands are the means by which we give ourselves to "the trusting and demanding God."[24] Instruction on God—the perfect Trinity—is a means by which the soul is opened to God's indwelling. Instruction is difficult to give and to receive, involving mortification and vivification

21. Gregory of Nyssa, *Christian Mode of Life*, 148.
22. Gregory of Nyssa, *Christian Mode of Life*, 152.
23. Gregory of Nyssa, *Christian Mode of Life*, 152.
24. Gregory of Nyssa, *Christian Mode of Life*, 154.

of heart, soul, and mind. But when we suffer divine teaching, we appear before God as ones more rather than less worthy of him. We strive to appear worthy, like those wedding guests commanded in Matthew 22:1–14. These guests wore wedding robes. We are all invited to the wedding banquet that is the new Jerusalem. We prepare for this by being perfect, pure and without guile before the Lord God Almighty.

The doctrine of God has form. It must express certain truths—most obviously, for our purposes in this chapter, God's perfection. Furthermore, its presentation of perfection, its form and voice, must be suitable to divine perfection. In the biblical testimony, perfection is first imperative and only then indicative. Doctrine is not, then, simply an indicative affair. It also contains an imperative. Robert Louis Wilken puts it this way: "Life and doctrine are immediately one."[25] Notice the order: life and then doctrine. "Be holy"—life—is one with the "I am holy" (Lev. 11:45).

That is one reason that Augustine's *Confessions* is so powerful. His description of his journey toward God gives rise to an enormously instructive doctrine of God. *Confessions* is not a doctrine of God—it is not *The Trinity*—but it is a work of unparalleled brilliance insofar as we see in it how "life and doctrine are immediately one." Augustine cannot know God until he begins to love him. Similarly, God's perfection will ring hollow until we become perfect ourselves. We must experience being perfect if we are to speak of God the perfect one. The aim of instruction in conceptual form is only preparatory. Its function, to use Wilken's words, is "to lead men and women to holiness of life."[26] The pure in heart will see God (Matt. 5:8). That they see is because God has given himself to be seen in faith and love in Jesus Christ.

The Father's Invisibility

Language of hearing may seem to have the upper hand in Scripture. "Faith is from hearing," writes Paul in Romans 10:17 (DBH). Yet sight

25. Robert Louis Wilken, *The Spirit of Early Christian Thought: Seeking the Face of God* (New Haven: Yale University Press, 2003), xiv.
26. Wilken, *Early Christian Thought*, xxii.

is a prevalent motif. Though the perfect Father is invisible, the perfect not only know but also desire him and his kingdom. Largeness of soul recognizes that just because something is invisible does not mean it is unintelligible. Moreover, the perfect—the pure—so delight in him that they see him with the eyes of their heart and soul. The perfect hear and delight so as to see. Accordingly, hearing ought not to be equated with seeing; rather, seeing is, I think, superior to hearing. Faith in what is heard is in the service of sight. We believe in order that we may see. If we, the perfect, are to be like angels, sight is indeed superior to faith. The angels do not believe in the Father but see the Father. We look forward to being like angels. What renders Gregory's saintly sister Macrina worthy of praise is, among other things, her being "attuned to an imitation of the existence of the angels." Like the angels, she led a life "divorced from all mortal vanity."[27] The angels, though discarnate and incorporeal, see the Father. Their life is one of ceaseless praise of what they see—hence their perfection. Our life, as it progresses on the path of discipleship, progresses in love of the unseen. Growth in faith is growth in sight.

God distributes his graces to those who have faith, or at least more than meager faith. "For to all those who have, more will be given, and they will have an abundance; but from those who have nothing, even what they have will be taken away" (Matt. 25:29). The material-minded are not like the angels, whereas the faithful are—"they cannot die anymore, because they are like angels and are children of God, being children of the resurrection" (Luke 20:36).[28] For the perfect, perception is not everything. Reality is better apprehended by largeness of soul. As Jesus teaches, it is what is inside the heart that matters. But those who are small of soul are not able to see "whence each of these things exist."[29] The small soul is unable to see even creaturely things as they are, as created. The pure in heart, the perfect, see in a manner that transcends the senses. They see that the one who

27. Gregory of Nyssa, *The Life of Saint Macrina*, in *Ascetical Works*, trans. Virginia Woods Callahan, ed. Roy Joseph Deferrari, Fathers of the Church (Washington, DC: Catholic University of America Press, 1967), 171.

28. Gregory of Nyssa, *Life of Saint Macrina*, 190.

29. Gregory of Nyssa, *On the Soul and the Resurrection*, in *Ascetical Works*, trans. Virginia Woods Callahan, ed. Roy Joseph Deferrari, Fathers of the Church (Washington, DC: Catholic University of America Press, 1967), 202.

comes in the likeness of sinful flesh and dies an ignominious death is God's Son, the Savior of the world. Sense perception is not the measure of everything. This is not to castigate the senses. Rather, as with created things in general, the senses' function is to guide, lead, and point to their Creator. One who is large in soul "sees through the eyes and uses what is known by the senses as guides and, in this way, penetrates from the visible to the invisible."[30] Faith hears, but in the life of the world to come, the believer sees. The invisible God will be seen to be "all in all." In this life, the perfect are not content with hearing. Instead, they hear in order that they may see Jesus Christ. In beholding Jesus, in seeing him, they know him as one with his invisible and perfect Father. Regenerate vision is equal to Jesus's vision. Jesus Christ sees his Father's angels; he receives their help in his temptations. When the Christian sees with Jesus, she sees the present angels, and joins with them, as she gathers around the Lord's Table, in praise of their Lord. She sees, to use Origen's memorable words, the presence of "a double church," angelic and human, invisible and visible.[31]

When our sight is regenerate, Scripture lives anew. Think for a moment of 1 Samuel 6:12: we hear of the untrained cows to whom the ark of the covenant is yoked as going "straight in the direction of Beth-shemesh along one highway," turning "neither to the right nor to the left" as they proceed toward Israelite territory. The cattle see as the Lord would have them see. The very power of God governs everything, encompassing even the cattle on their way to Beth-shemesh. Regenerate sight is the gift of the intelligible and invisible God.

Perfection, on the creature's part, is activated in the soul. Our souls are perfect not only in the trust that leads to understanding but also in the sight that is completed in love. The soul that is perfect exhibits a reasonable symmetry between its archetype (God) and itself. Perfect creaturely intelligence desires the one who is intelligence itself: God who knows and wills himself in relation to nothing outside himself. "So, if some quality is not recognized as part of the divine nature, we cannot reasonably think that it is part of the nature of the soul."[32]

---

30. Gregory of Nyssa, *Soul and the Resurrection*, 207.
31. Origen, *Homily on Luke 23:8*, cited in Wilken, *Early Christian Thought*, 48.
32. Gregory of Nyssa, *Soul and the Resurrection*, 217.

We see that the life of the perfect is not simply one of correspondence between them and the Lord. It is a matter of the perfect God being in the perfect creature, the archetype in the image. This does not collapse the two, and it does not compromise the very great difference between the two. Remember, God does not gain anything from being in us, though the reverse is not true—we receive life. We progress, becoming more ourselves in relation to God rather than less. To be perfect is a matter of being true to our essence as those made in God's image and to achieve likeness to God, our beginning and end. In looking to Jesus Christ—who is the image of God—we are not only declared but also made perfect. We become ourselves. Herein I think it acceptable to say that God is mingled—though not confused, as it were—with us. When we are perfect, there is nothing in us that is not of him. God pervades us: we become coincident with God. The Lord God contains in an essential sense what exists in us by his grace. There exists in us nothing that he is not. We are fully restored to his image and transformed in relation to his likeness.

Insofar as we are conformed to God's image, Jesus Christ, the church's teaching on God experiences renewed vigor. The objective perfection of God encourages the subjective perfection of the theologian—indeed of all Christians. There arises a renewed sense of the terrifying holiness and goodness of God. Inhabitation of Christian truth becomes the means by which we become like God, made new in accordance with the image of Jesus Christ. Likeness to the perfect God: that is a gift of God. But it is not from God in a way that obviates our striving. Relentless obedience to Jesus Christ, the turning to him in faith—this leads to our renewal and perfection. To the extent that we turn, our moral lives resemble what is ontologically true of us—that we are in Jesus Christ and baptized by his Spirit.

When an account of God's life is pursued in an exegetical and devotional mode, it knows no food and drink other than the Scriptures. The conceptual form, which is to be scriptural through and through, must have devotional import. Wilken writes of Hilary of Poitiers's *The Trinity* that it "breathes a spirit of devotion."[33] Theology, then,

---

33. Wilken, *Early Christian Thought*, 87. The same, of course, could be said of other great works in the tradition—for example, Calvin's *Institutes*.

cannot be done well without experience of the dominical command. Personal experience of the command—our making progress in the perfection commanded of us—matters. Likewise, the personal is never isolated from the ecclesial. In the community of the crucified, we sing God's praises, pray, confess sins, receive absolution, hear the Word, receive it sacramentally, and serve Christ in "the least of these" (Matt. 25:45). This, too, contributes to our perfection. Without these things, the conceptual form of Christian teaching ossifies instead of yielding love. Without our immersion in the church's sacramental life, its worship and prayer, Scripture does not yield its full treasure. We fail to see and receive its treasure. Similarly, theology loses touch with its anchor, Scripture, and its end, God, when its ecclesial setting is ignored.

In short, we can be perfect only insofar as we "see the Holy Trinity," and we see only insofar as we love the Father and Son in the love that is the Spirit.[34] The perfect Father never ceases to love his Son, the Son the Father, and all that in the Spirit. The Spirit, as the bond of their love, makes it possible for us to love them. The Spirit encourages desire for things above, for the archetype of perfection itself, the Father. The Spirit fills us with the love of the Father for the Son and the Son for the Father, enabling us to dwell in their love. The Spirit's ministry is so extraordinarily fruitful that we are actually capable of imitating what is above and naturally inaccessible to us. The Spirit binds us to the Son and in him to the Father in such a way that what is common to them by nature is ours by grace. The Spirit makes perfection, what Gregory calls "complete assimilation to the divine," actual.[35]

When we are perfect, we see only what is good. We no longer desire sin and are no longer bewitched by evil. Disobedience holds no appeal. We desire only more of what we love—that is to say, God. With the psalmist we say, "I have no good apart from you" (Ps. 16:2). Our life is thus in God and not ourselves, which is the only way to truly exist as the creatures we are. Perfection is convertible, then, with existence. The perfect is goodness itself, and "what actually exists

34. Wilken, *Early Christian Thought*, 108.
35. Gregory of Nyssa, *Soul and the Resurrection*, 238.

is the nature of the good." What exists is good, and what is good is perfect. In addition, in keeping with our previous chapter on God's manner of existence, when we obey Jesus, we "become simple and uncomplex and god-like." Accordingly, we discover "the only thing in existence which is absolutely delectable and loveable."[36] The perfect do not cling to themselves but to God. With Paul, they consider all else "as loss because of Christ. More than that, [they] regard everything as loss because of the surpassing value of knowing Christ Jesus [their] Lord" (Phil. 3:7–8). Being perfect is not a rigid state of being. The perfect love God in their movement and act. And they do so in relation to "the least of these." Because of their "God-loving life," they are not self-conscious of their ministering to Christ in and through the least.[37] "Perfect love," says 1 John 4:18, "casts out fear." The perfect live and move in relationship to God and in intimacy with the least.

There is also an aesthetic dimension to consider. God's beauty draws us to God. We come to love God because God "is, by nature, beautiful."[38] The perfect is beautiful. When we love God, we become perfect and so share in God's beauty. Those who are perfect are never content, however, with how much they love God, for the divine life in all its terrifying beauty never ceases to satisfy. The perfect want to love more. Love for God never reaches a plateau. The Perfect One never satiates the perfect; the beautiful draws us ever onward.

A Light Yoke

The call to perfection is not a heavy burden. It represents, rather, a light yoke. It is much better than sin. Sin deforms us; it is the very antithesis of our nature. We are not created as sinners. We are profoundly restless creatures, seeking, sinful as we are, our own gods. The perfection of God is archetypal, and we necessarily long to return to our source, though we rarely return in the right ways. The perfection to which we are called and which is our true home is that to which Jesus calls us and that to which he brings us, pure and spotless. We

36. Gregory of Nyssa, *Soul and the Resurrection*, 239.
37. Gregory of Nyssa, *Christian Mode of Life*, 152.
38. Gregory of Nyssa, *Soul and the Resurrection*, 240.

can heed Christ's call to be perfect and to free ourselves from vice by calling on him—"I believe; help my unbelief!" (Mark 9:24). This is much better than sin.

When we participate in God's perfection, we become "larger and more receptive to that in which it exists."[39] Perfection is not only true of God but is God himself, indicative of the manner in which God exists. Similarly, it is our nature to be without blemish and fault. We are (again) created "very good" (Gen. 1:31). As we obey the Sermon on the Mount, we do not diminish but rather increase, becoming "more receptive." Gregory recognizes that we who participate in the divine good shall always grow and never cease to grow.[40] If we chose to obey Christ's command and be perfect as is his Father, we become perfect. We become what we choose. When we choose God, we become more rather than less inclusive of God.

God's perfection is restorative, making us "divine."[41] By that we simply mean that it restores our nature to us, which was originally divine in that there was nothing in us that was not of God. This is, as we have seen, not to conflate the radical dissimilarity between God and creatures. But it is to say that our nature was originally pure, a pure likeness of our archetype, God, and thus compatible with him. Perfection is "the fulfillment of our nature."[42] To be fulfilled as a creature is to be our true selves. We hope to be, by being perfect, what we were in the beginning—those who walked with God. In this life, then, we are to walk with God, living "in love, as Christ loved us" (Eph. 5:2). In so doing we cultivate virtue, becoming the kinds of persons who grow into a perfect plant.[43]

Without either perfection or purity of heart, what is said of Solomon cannot be said of us: he "loved the LORD, walking in the statutes of his father David" (1 Kings 3:3). Solomon knew the statutes to be of God, God's gift to his people mediated through David. God's love is perfect, "whose service is perfect freedom," as the Prayer for Peace in the Book of Common Prayer has it. The perfection of which Jesus

---

39. Gregory of Nyssa, *Soul and the Resurrection*, 244.
40. See further Gregory of Nyssa, *Soul and the Resurrection*, 245.
41. Gregory of Nyssa, *Soul and the Resurrection*, 265.
42. Gregory of Nyssa, *Soul and the Resurrection*, 267.
43. See further Gregory of Nyssa, *Soul and the Resurrection*, 271.

speaks is profoundly moral; the perfect honors the love of God. And yet we cannot know, let alone love, the perfect God without being perfect ourselves, without walking in the statutes. We learn to see the Perfect One as he is by imitating him, living in love. Ever-increasing degrees of purity perfect sight. "Where there is love, there is seeing," writes Richard of Saint Victor.[44]

Conclusion

I cannot give an account of God's names without pointing to the forms of life necessary to receiving his names. When we consider the dominical call, we must remember that Christ helps in the Spirit those who hear his command. He does not leave us without himself. He frees us from what enslaves us, but not without us. We must struggle against sin, recognizing that the struggle "takes place in every human soul visited by grace."[45] An account of God's perfection must prescribe practice. Once again, the "be" comes before the "is." When you are perfect, you will confess that your Father is perfect. The essential names of God have this characteristic feature, that of a double perspective: teaching and practice, indication and imperative.

When we look at Jesus, we see the Father's perfection; when we look at him, we see goodness. We see that in his human face there is something that cannot be seen, God's form (see Phil. 2:6). When we look at Jesus, who commands us to be perfect, we see the living perfection of God. We do not, however, stand passive before him; we follow him. If we look at the sun for more than a few seconds, we will go blind.[46] Similarly, we do not stare at Jesus; we follow Jesus and his commands. To see him is to follow him in a program of moral and spiritual renewal.

In this book, I write an account of the Christian life in relation to truths of God's being. God's existence and the way in which he exists encourage a particular form of life. My contention is that the names described in this book are shortchanged if the form of life

44. Quoted in Wilken, *Early Christian Thought*, 184.
45. Wilken, *Early Christian Thought*, 233.
46. See Wilken, *Early Christian Thought*, 260.

they engender is ignored.[47] Think, for example, of Paul's exhortation in 2 Corinthians 7:1: "Let us purify ourselves from every pollution of flesh and spirit, perfecting holiness in fear of God" (DBH). We cannot hear of God's perfection without receiving it as a "perfecting holiness." Even stronger, following Hebrews 12:14, without perfection "no one will see the Lord." We cannot see him if we forsake his commands. The doctrine of God is an orientation, though it is not only that. It involves teaching and practice related to an end, which is God. As Wilken notes, "Whether the term is *perfection* or *holiness*, the New Testament presents Christian faith as life oriented toward an end, toward a goal, what in the language of ancient moral philosophy was called the final good, the *summum bonum*."[48] By believing certain divine things, Christians become certain kinds of persons, perfect and holy persons. The theological life is complementary to the moral and religious life. We progress in understanding insofar as we are like God and follow Jesus.[49]

But we must pause for a warning. Theology must never be thought of as an exercise in doctrinal athleticism.[50] Indeed, part of the aim of this book is to encourage piety and affection. The language of the heart is coextensive with the metaphysics of God. Wilken again: "Nothing is more characteristic of the Christian intellectual tradition than its fondness for the language of the heart."[51] We know only in love; we make progress in the truth by loving. The form of an account of God's names must encourage one to turn to God, to desire God even more. Be perfect—there is nothing better than being perfect as your Father in heaven is perfect.

Serene objectivity, indeed austerity, is not always beneficial to presentations of holy teaching. When we love, we enjoy; we also desire to share the fruits of our contemplation. As the doctors of the church universally recognize, knowledge of God is deeply participatory. To know the perfect God is to be perfect. The form of teaching on God must invite participation and encourage communion, spur "restless

---

47. See Wilken, *Early Christian Thought*, 264.
48. Wilken, *Early Christian Thought*, 272.
49. See Wilken, *Early Christian Thought*, 275.
50. See Wilken, *Early Christian Thought*, 278.
51. Wilken, *Early Christian Thought*, 292.

movement toward God."[52] It is a matter of thinking by seeking, knowing by loving, of becoming perfect.

In sum, the names treated in this book are a guide to the spiritual life. It is, as Wilken says of "the Christian intellectual tradition," "an exercise in thinking about the God who is known and seeking the One who is loved."[53] The enterprise involved in unfolding names common to the Three is at once "theological and spiritual," a matter of thinking so as to see. If an account of the perfect God is to be this, it must be "grounded in authentic religious experience."[54] Even stronger, it is a function of such experience. "The way to truth" not only "passes through the concrete and personal" but is sustained by the concrete and personal. The way to the truth regarding God's perfection is bound up with personal perfection. It simply assumes the Christian life. More boldly, the Christian life—the life of perfection—bears us in our consideration of the great truth of God. Personal perfection is the principle of intelligibility for knowing. We know the perfect God by being perfect. Though knowledge will one day "be made ineffectual," love will not (1 Cor. 13:8 DBH). Perfect love—this is our beginning, our present call, and our end.

52. Wilken, *Early Christian Thought*, 309.
53. Wilken, *Early Christian Thought*, 311.
54. Wilken, *Early Christian Thought*, 314.

4

Infinity and the Christian Life

Do I not fill heaven and earth? says the LORD.

—Jeremiah 23:24

To the extent that we grow in likeness to God, we enjoy a degree of relative infinity. Infinity is, of course, an idiom not found in the Bible, and yet it honors an indispensable biblical truth. What is that truth? Simply put, God's being is not determined by anything outside God. As Thomas writes, "God is His own subsistent being."[1] This indicates that God does not need anything outside himself in order to be.[2] God does "not exist in anything else."[3] The triune Lord does not have life in relation to anything other than himself. The Lord fills heaven and earth, as the Jeremiah text above indicates,[4] but does not need heaven and earth in order to be.

This teaching is at the heart of the biblical testimony. God not only creates heaven and earth but also fills them. However, God is

1. Thomas Aquinas, *Summa contra Gentiles* 2.52, trans. Fathers of the English Dominican Province (London: Burns, Oates, and Washbourne, 1924), 153.
2. Thomas Aquinas, *Summa Theologiae* (hereafter *ST*) I.7.1 (trans. Pegis, 1:57).
3. *ST* I.7.1, ad. 3 (trans. Pegis, 1:57).
4. Thomas cites this Scripture in his question on infinity. See *ST* I.8.2 (trans. Pegis, 1:65).

not contained by what he fills. The Lord is present, intimately present, to all that he causes. He is present to all things as their cause. The Lord is present, moreover, as the Infinite One. My concern in the first section of this chapter has to do with whether infinity is in any sense communicable to creatures to which God is present. Is infinity a name or attribute that may be shared by creatures that are not by nature infinite? Dust that we are, is it God's intention that we share—somehow—in his infinity?

Angelic Existence

To think clearly about this, Thomas encourages us to look to the angels. Angelic existence is important for determining how human creatures participate in God's infinity. Thomas notes that the angels are "self-subsisting." Their existence is such that they "are not received into matter."[5] Angels are discarnate creatures enjoying a nonmaterial form of existence.[6] In discussing the nature of angelic existence, Thomas introduces a key phrase that is useful for our purposes. He says of the angels that they are "relatively infinite."[7] This is an important insight. Angels are created beings. And though they are not absolutely infinite as is God, they possess relative infinity, meaning their infinity derives from God, not themselves. We need to wrestle with this. May the relative infinity of the angels be one day proper to us? And what is the Holy Spirit's role in rendering us into the sorts of people who are capable of receiving infinity, albeit relatively?

To proceed faithfully, it would be wise to consider our creatureliness. We are creatures. We are produced. We are not God. Instead, we are from God. God is our "first principle."[8] Because we are from God, we have what Thomas calls a "determinate nature."[9] That nature will never be shed. We are visible creatures, embodied souls made in the

5. *ST* I.7.2 (trans. Pegis, 1:58).
6. Notably, Paul Griffiths expresses dissatisfaction with Thomas at this point. This is because Thomas abstracts "the angels altogether from the body." Thomas does not consider that angels are capable "of spatio-temporal location." See *Decreation: The Last Things of All Creatures* (Waco: Baylor University Press, 2014), 128, 122.
7. *ST* I.7.2 (trans. Pegis, 1:58).
8. *ST* I.7.2, s.c. (trans. Pegis, 1:58).
9. *ST* I.7.2 (trans. Pegis, 1:58).

image and being restored to the likeness of God. Even in the life of the world to come, we will have bodies. God, however, is bodiless, invisible. "God is spirit" (John 4:24).

How can we who are bodily beings receive infinity? Is infinitely really communicable? After all, we are not "self-subsisting," as is the case with angels. Is there a way forward? Yes, I think so. The way forward begins in a seemingly unlikely place, with what Origen calls a "divine sense."[10] We must, in other words, think about what kinds of persons we must become. The infinite and almighty "God and Father of our Lord Jesus Christ" (2 Cor. 11:31) is a bodiless and intellectual being. In order to receive him as the Father, we must advance beyond bodily senses to a divine sense. How do we acquire a divine sense? And what is the fruit of such a sense?

God makes us in such a way that we may share in him. God's manner of being is communicable. A name like infinity is, to put it technically, a participatable name. How do we receive a share in God's infinity? The more we love God, the greater is the degree of our participation in not only all that is his but also the manner in which it is his. God is love, infinitely so. The more we adhere to him, the greater is our share in his infinite goodness, beauty, truth, and love. This is what Origen means by a "divine sense." "Loving affection" is at the heart of such a sense, and its blessing is "a participation in himself."[11]

Knowledge and sight are intimately related to each other. The world, says Jesus of the invisible Spirit, "neither sees him nor knows him" (John 14:17). The disciples, however, do know the Spirit, but they do not see the Spirit who abides in them. In the life of the world to come, the disciples will see the Father and the Son. We, too, will see. We will also know, but know in love. Love is the perfection of knowledge. Knowledge and love, while distinct in this life, are "one and the same in the next."[12]

Stephen's martyrdom is exemplary of the pedagogy I am sketching. Because he is "filled with the Holy Spirit," he gazes into heaven and sees "the glory of God and Jesus standing at the right hand of

10. Origen, *On First Principles* 1.1.9, ed. and trans. John Behr (Oxford: Oxford University Press, 2017), 1:39.
11. Behr's introduction to Origen, *On First Principles*, 1:lxvii.
12. Behr's introduction to Origen, *On First Principles*, 1:lxxxviii.

God" (Acts 7:55). He sees the heavens open (Acts 7:56). Stephen's place "in the heavenly court" will be an exalted one.[13] Stephen will not be one of those whom Paul describes as being saved, "but only as through fire" (1 Cor. 3:15). His heavenly treasures are abundant. The degree to which he sees will be superior to many. Stephen received a participation in God in this life. This participation enabled him to see, in this life, the glory of God and Jesus standing at God's right hand.

To sum up what has been said: God is infinite, meaning that God is not contained by what is not God. We are not infinite, for we are from God. In order to participate in God, we must acquire a divine sense. Such a sense involves love. The more we love, the more we receive and the greater is our participation in the God who is unseen. Accordingly, I think it appropriate to talk about our receiving a relative infinity. To advance our contemplation of this matter, we must more deeply consider the Holy Spirit, who makes us capable of receiving "a participation in God."

The Bodiless God

Infinity is identical to the one God. God is good and God is love. God is all that he is. God's essential names, all God's attributes, are convertible with himself. When we talk about participating in God, we are thinking in an essential register. We are talking about a sharing in all that is common to the Three and in their manner of being.[14]

We have earthly bodies. Our bodies are by their very nature local. To be a body is to be somewhere, not everywhere. Is there any integrity, then, to our participating in the bodiless God? Since God is not a body, God is therefore everywhere and not contained by anything. God, says Origen in *On First Principles*, is "unspeakably and immeasurably superior" to all that is not God.[15] To describe God's infinity, then, is to unfold his superiority to all that is created, things visible

13. Behr's introduction to Origen, *On First Principles*, 1:lxxxviii.
14. Note that we do not share in the relations of origin. For example, we do not share in the Father's begetting of the Son, but we do share in the one essence common to them.
15. Origen, *On First Principles* 1.1.5. Hereafter *FP* and cited in text.

and invisible. That said, we understand something of his superiority through "the beauty of his works" (FP 1.1.6). Creatures are able to behold the Infinite One through his works. More than that, creatures are able to know him. We are able to understand "the divine doctrines, which are manifestly bodiless" (FP 1.1.7). The finite is made in such a way that it can perceive and understand its cause, the infinite God. But the question remains, Can the finite participate in the infinite? Can what is finite by nature enjoy a degree of relative infinity? Origen rightly insists that we do wrong to understand God "by means of bodily nature" (FP 1.1.7). God is not as we are; God is not a greater version of ourselves. We are composite creatures, whereas God is not. We are "a concurrence of body and soul" (FP 1.1.6), whereas God is not composed of anything, invisible by his very nature.

Though God is bodiless, God sees. Scripture talks in lavish terms about God's sight. "Who can hide in secret places so that I cannot see them? says the LORD" (Jer. 23:24). Sight describes God's relationship to what he causes. He sees us but does not see himself. In terms of the inner divine life, knowledge prevails. God knows himself. "No one knows the Son except the Father, and no one knows the Father except the Son and anyone to whom the Son chooses to reveal him" (Matt. 11:27). The Father and Son do not see each other. Each knows and is known "through the faculty of knowledge" (FP 1.1.8). Because God is an intellectual being and subsists in relation to himself, the faculty of knowledge—and not sight—is most appropriate to the Father-Son relationship. When it comes to God's relation to the created order, sight is most relevant.

God knows himself and sees us. Following Origen's lead, to see "God in the heart . . . [is] to understand and to know him with the intellect" (FP 1.1.9). We "see with the eyes of the heart" and know him with "the intellect." God, however, does not know and see as we do. We do not see in secret, whereas God does. God's sight is divine; it is neither mortal nor corruptible. Importantly, when we see with the eyes of the heart, what Origen calls "divine sense," we see in an "immortal and intellectual way" (FP 1.1.9). If our heart is pure, we truly see; we see as God sees. We see the Immortal One and know him intellectually. The home of divine sense is the heart, and a pure heart is synonymous with a pure intellect.

We must not think that Origen is merely juxtaposing the heart and the intellect. Rather, he equates them. The "intellectual faculty," Origen writes, "is indeed called *heart*." We see by the heart. This, Origen thinks, is the abundant testimony of "all the Scriptures, both old and new" (*FP* 1.1.9). How do we cultivate heart and sight and thus our "intellectual faculty"? How do we nurture a divine sense? What kind of spiritual pedagogy does God's infinity encourage? The divine sense is cultivated by looking upon Jesus Christ, "the *splendour*" (*FP* 1.2.8) of the Father. How do we, distracted as we are and scandalized by his form, look upon Jesus Christ? And how does such looking upon Christ contribute to our understanding of infinity as communicable?

Origen offers some helpful hints. He once again uses the motif of participation. He argues that creatures participate in the Father simply by existing. Existence is a gift of the Father. All things are from him, the giver of existence. Creatures *are* because he *is*. In terms of the Son, Origen notes, "All who are rational beings are partakers of the Word of God, that is Reason." The Son is Reason.[16] Rational beings participate in the Son. "Christ," says Origen, "is in the hearts of all in respect of his being the Word or Reason" (*FP* 1.3.6). This is true of all persons. All "have a participation in God" (*FP* 1.3.6). Their being as rational creatures is their participation.

Not all are Christians, however. Just because all partake of him, all are not said to be his people. Origen, it seems to me, shows that our creation has reference to the Son. Simply by being, rational creatures such as ourselves participate in the one through whom we are. This general "working of the power of God the Father and of the Son [is] extended without distinction over every creature" (*FP* 1.3.7). The claim being made here is fairly minimal. Creatures share in their cause. Creatures participate, simply by being creatures, in the Father and the Son. Human beings are created in such a way that we participate in the Father and Son: the Father by existing, the Son in terms of our being rational creatures. Note, however, that we do not all participate (fully) in the Spirit. Participation in the Spirit does not apply

16. He is also described as Wisdom and Justice. See Origen, *On First Principles* 1.3.6.

in a general sense to human beings. Only "the holy ones," writes Origen, possess "participation in the Holy Spirit" (*FP* 1.3.7). There is, you might say, a general and low-level participation in the Spirit. All "terrestrial and bodily things," indeed "all" that would walk on the earth, participate in the life-giving Spirit (*FP* 1.3.4). Recall the creedal language: the Spirit is the life-giver; the Spirit gives life to all that is. However, only the holy ones are said to possess a participation in the Holy Spirit. Only the holy ones are truly intimate with the Spirit. All things participate in a general sense in the Spirit as the principle of life, but only the holy may be said to possess the Spirit. Indeed, there is a crucial distinction to be made between participating in the Spirit in a general sense and having the Spirit bestowed upon one through the waters of baptism (see *FP* 1.3.7). Those who enjoy the bestowed Spirit are men and women who, through ever-increasing purity and cleanliness of life, "more worthily receive" that same Spirit.

Cast in terms of the Pauline language of justification and sanctification, our justification in Christ removes all stains of original pollution, and our sanctification in Christ (and the Spirit) compels us to advance in what we have received "such as to be worthy of God." God makes us pure and perfect in Jesus Christ. But we must become worthy of the one who makes us thus. Such worthiness is received in the Spirit. The Spirit makes us "purer and cleaner" (*FP* 1.3.8). We are by the Spirit enabled to make "so great an advance in cleanliness and purity" (*FP* 1.3.8). The Spirit is the key to unfolding how we share in what exceeds us.

The Trinitarian Dimension

The trinitarian reference here is strong. The Lord Jesus instructs and trains us. He leads us "on to perfection by strengthening and unceasing sanctification of the Holy Spirit." Jesus declares us perfect and leads us, in his Spirit, to perfection. He does so by the Spirit's "unceasing sanctification." If we are unceasingly sanctified, we "attain God" (*FP* 1.3.8). In attaining God, we attain relative infinity. Here we arrive at the heart of the matter. Without the Spirit's unceasing sanctification, the Spirit's cultivation of a divine sense, we can neither attain nor receive God's manner of being. Infinity is attainable in relation to the Spirit. This is God's work all the way down. We may make progress toward God, and if we do, by virtue of much exertion, we know that it is only through "the ceaseless working" of God the Spirit (*FP* 1.3.8).

As we "behold the holy and blessed life, we ought so to continue," writes Origen, "that no satiety of that good should ever seize us." When we consider the blessed life, its vistas are unending and infinite. Because God's Spirit gives us a share in God's infinity, we shall never tire of that infinity. The Spirit will continue to bestow blessedness and happiness, inexhaustibly so. Accordingly, the more we receive God's infinite goodness and holiness, "the more the desire for it in us should be expanded and extended" (*FP* 1.3.8). The expansion of desire in us is the work of infinity. Herein we see, once again, infinity's bearing on Christian life. Christian life, as perfected in the life of the world to come, shall forever be perfected. God in his infinity, in his infinite goodness and love, shall never allow his creatures to become full, bored, or satiated, as it were. God is not expanding and extending, but we who attain the Father and the Son in the Spirit will ceaselessly grow. Our blessedness will know no end, for it is an ever-increasing blessedness in relation to the one whose blessedness is unbounded.

This is, in part, what I think it means to follow Paul when he writes in 1 Corinthians 15:28, "So that God may be all in all." If God the Spirit is in us, and it is God the Spirit who brings us to the Father in the Son forever and ever, then we do make progress in heaven. Our desire to see "face to face" (1 Cor. 13:12), because the one seen is so great, shall ever grow. The correlate of God's being "all in all" is an infinite desire for God. God's infinity grounds heavenly bliss, world without end. Though there are not stages of progress in the life to come, there is ever-increasing intensity of desire, corresponding to God's infinity.

The work of the Spirit in this is plain. To "be filled with the Spirit" (Eph. 5:18) means to be filled by the infinite Spirit. We will not shed our spiritual bodies, but we will have shed our mortal bodies. We will enjoy a new kind of corporeality about which it is impossible to speak. Our bodies will experience an infinite manner of existence. In the life of the world to come, the infinite Spirit will permeate our bodies. The infinite Spirit will infinitely draw us to the Son, who will be bodily visible, glorified wounds and all. As we gaze on him in the new heavens and earth, God (the Father) shall be all in all, filling all with joy unending.

Here again, we are back to where we began. We return to the divine life, God's manner of being. Origen reminds us that God's infinity is essential, meaning that it is proper to God, Father, Son, and Holy Spirit. God is, and will always be, infinite and uncontained. God does not acquire infinity. God experiences neither increase nor decrease. This is true with respect to other names—for example, goodness. The infinity that we receive, however, is accidental in nature. Infinity will never be proper to us. Infinity will be ours in the life of the world to come, but ours as creatures. Infinity is, as Origen notes of holiness, "an accidental quality in every created being" (*FP* 1.5.5). Infinite existence is a gift.

Paraenesis will no longer be relevant in the life of the world to come. We shall not be able to fall from God. Conflicts and struggles with the adversary and his servants—these things shall have passed. Our faculties will have been utterly transformed. Our sight will experience "a kind of change and transformation of form." The eschatological remaking of heaven and earth involves "the transmutation of the form of this world" (*FP* 1.6.4). This world will be fit for infinity. Again, the infinite shall, following 1 Corinthians 15:28, be "all in all." How this will be, we do not know. But our transmutation involves an expansion of ourselves, a stretching out, as it were. It will be impossible to grow weary of heavenly treasures. The Spirit will not cease to bind us to the glorious Son and in him to the Father, communicating their life. The life of the infinite Father will be in us through the infinite Son by the immeasurable Spirit who is their love (see John 17:26). The infinitely holy Spirit will always ensure that we who are not "substantially holy" never cease to love and enjoy him who is "substantially holy" (*FP* 1.8.3).

The end is better than the beginning. No bad will be allowed in. There is only the tree of life (see Rev. 22:2, 14). We will discern, know, and love all in the Spirit. Ceaseless receiving of the gifts of the Spirit—this is the life of the world to come. The Spirit comprehends the Father's infinity and will not cease to share the depths of that with us. Indeed, we shall, in the Spirit, ceaselessly search the depths of the Father, inexhaustible as they are. All of eternity will not yield the fullness of those depths. Even as we, with the angels, "continually see the face of [Jesus's] Father in heaven" (Matt. 18:10), that seeing will never result in apathy. For what is seen gives more and more appetite to what is unseen. The Lord Jesus Christ, "the last Adam," the "life-giving spirit" (1 Cor. 15:45), will never cease to minister the Spirit, and the Spirit will never cease to minister spiritual life. As Paul writes, "We will bear the image of the man of heaven" (1 Cor. 15:49).

God as Ever Greater

Though we shall bear Christ's image, we shall never be his equals; we will, however, be his friends. He shall always remain greater. The Creator-creature relation is irreversible and has consequences throughout eternity. The Lord Jesus will never receive from us in an ontological sense, though we shall always receive the infinite and life-giving Spirit from him. And we shall only want to receive and worship him. In this life, of course, we do not always desire him. Rather than cooperate with him, we resist him. In the next life, we shall always cooperate. It will never occur to us to will otherwise than God, for we shall see that there is nothing better. Again, as those who will be with our Lord in a house with "many dwelling places" (John 14:2), our hunger and desire for him shall never come to an end. The hunger for God that prayerfully marks the faithful in this life will mark them in heaven. As Paul Murray says of Thomas's account of prayer, "From this hunger [for God] there follows abundance of everlasting life."[17]

From this hunger for God there follows sight. The one seen will satisfy us in such a way that we shall be "purified to resplendence," as Origen says. Here we reach the heart of the matter. Will we, those one day to be "purified to resplendence," see God the Father (FP 2.3.6)? God's nature is "invisible," as Paul reminds us in Romans 1:20, but may the person of the Father be seen in heaven? Can believers who receive relative infinity see the person of the Father in the life to come? Let us proceed with care in sketching a response.

17. Paul Murray, OP, *Praying with Confidence: Aquinas on the Lord's Prayer* (London: Continuum, 2010), 70.

Thomas reminds us that "*nature* designates the principle of action."[18] God creates something good because God is good. God is invisible, and yet we see glimpses of his goodness in things made. We cannot see God's invisible nature apart from things made. In this life, we must imitate God, for imitation cleanses sight. We do not see him with bodily eyes, to be sure, but we do see the Father with the eyes of the heart. Recall that Origen talks about "understanding him [the Father] with the vision of the heart and the perception of the mind, and this only in part." In other words, we may in this life understand the Father with "the vision of the heart" (*FP* 2.4.3). In the life to come, I think that we will see the Father insofar as the Father is all in all. We will not see the one essence common to the Three. However, we will see the Father himself and his Son and Spirit, one God, and therefore the Godhead common to them. The Father's very being will be seen through all things. "We will see him as he is" (1 John 3:2), the infinitely beautiful, loving, and good God, "the God and Father of the Lord Jesus Christ" (2 Cor. 11:31).

In loving him and obeying, we are made fit to receive him as he makes himself known. One day God the Father will be manifest to the obedient and seen as he is. Let us think further about this. The infinite God makes a good and finite world whose form will one day pass. The form of the world as we know it will pass when God the Father gathers "up all things in him [Christ], things in heaven and things on earth" (Eph. 1:10). Following the first article of the creed, power is said to be true of the Father almighty as Creator of heaven and earth, of all things seen and unseen. Power is an essential name appropriated to the Father. This name is the principle of the Father's action in creation. Recall again Thomas's point regarding the "nature" of God's power. Power is true of the Father's nature, understood as the principle of action for creating. The Father's power is seen in the things that are made. The Father's power is seen with "the vision of the heart" (*FP* 2.4.3). In addition, our Father, who is in heaven, will one day be on earth too, the new earth, just as he will be in the new heaven, which will contain earth afresh. When we talk about seeing the Father, I think we have to talk on the level of what is said

18. *ST* I.39.2, ad. 3 (trans. Pegis, 1:366).

of him in relation to Son and Spirit. This is the salience, in part, of seeing him as he is, as always in relation to Son and Spirit. We shall see God the Father, Son, and Spirit and all things in relationship to them. In seeing them, we see their essence and experience their nature.

The Love of God

We must endeavor to connect and deepen this basic insight with respect to the Holy Spirit, "Who is Love." We shall one day see the love that the Spirit is.[19] We shall not see the Spirit in an embodied sense, for the Holy Spirit is spirit, but we shall see the love that the Spirit is in the Father and Son. Love stands for the person of the Spirit. The Holy Spirit is love. Love is also an essential name, for love is proper to the essence common to the Three. The kind of ever-increasing "affectionate intimacy" is an intimacy with the Three.[20] The ministry of the Spirit in the life of the world to come is to ever expand our sight, infinitely so. We shall never cease to see. Our sight will grow neither dull nor dim. The life of the world to come is life "beyond all measure" (2 Cor. 4:17), the infinite life of the Father, Son, and Spirit. We shall look and see "what cannot be seen" (2 Cor. 4:18). We shall walk in and by the Spirit. The Spirit is our "pledge" in this life, and will be evermore (Eph. 1:14). And what the Spirit guarantees is a home, our heavenly dwelling, "a house not made with hands, eternal in the heavens" (2 Cor. 5:1). This is a house where the Lord is, a house that is not contained by anything.

There is much to see in this life that we cannot now see. Because of our frailty, we "can neither see everything by the eye nor comprehend everything by reason" (*FP* 2.6.1). When we love God, however, our sight is renewed. We acquire the "divine sense." We see for the first time. We see "the image of the invisible God," Jesus Christ (Col. 1:15). We also begin to love those whom no one sees. "Lord, when was it that we saw you hungry or thirsty or a stranger or naked or sick or in prison, and did not take care of you?" (Matt. 25:44). Accordingly,

19. *ST* I.39.8 (trans. Pegis, 1:380).
20. Thomas Aquinas, *Compendium theologiae* 2, 194, cited in Murray, *Praying with Confidence*, 100.

we enjoy a participation in God. We are united to God, joined to God through love, not simply by our loving but by the Spirit, who is love. By the powerful working of the Spirit, we love and so we see.

This raises an important question. Will we cease to have a will in heaven? If I understand Origen correctly, his answer is no. He writes, "The firmness of purpose and immensity of affection and inextinguishable warmth of love" destroy "all thought of alteration or change, such that what was dependent upon the will is now changed into nature by the exertion of long usage" (*FP* 2.6.5). This seems about right to me. Our will becomes one with our nature; God is our all in all, the all of everything in the world to come. Since we will be in the Word and Spirit forever, and thus in the Father forever, we will be God. This is true insofar as all that we do, feel, and understand will be immutably God. The warmth of our love will ceaselessly increase and expand, all because of our union with the Word in the Spirit (see *FP* 2.6.6). This is not to suggest for a moment that we are somehow swallowed up into God. No, we remain creatures, but we will be so proximate to God that the very nature of our bodies will be changed. We will see. We will be so transformed by love of the unseen that the distinctions between our intellect, our will, and our sight will be utterly relativized.

The Christian life involves will, and profoundly so. Our will may progress toward God or defect from God. We are called to imitate God, though often we do not. The more we imitate God, the more we love God. The more we love, the more we merit treasures in the world to come. Those whose warmth of love burns ever warmer in this life will not be as those whose works are burned up. Just as some in this life experience a greater intimacy with the Lord, so too will some in the next. All will see, but some will see with a greater intensity than others.

Sight has the greatest salience, biblically speaking. Just as Paul in 1 Corinthians 13 says that love is greater than faith and hope, sight has a greater density than either knowing or willing. Time and time again Scripture speaks of God's face, whether in the heavenly courtroom scene of Job 1:11 or Jesus's declaration that the angels of the "little ones . . . continually see the face of my Father in heaven" (Matt. 18:10). We see the infinite God in this life through "*purity of heart*"; that is how we know him (*FP* 2.11.7). In this life, we see with the heart. In the life to come, our sight will merge with our nature in ways we are unable now to describe. Possessing spiritual bodies, we shall see God and be seen without measure, enjoying a lack of constraints. His infinite life will be ours, then, in that we shall always see him as he is. He will no longer be in heaven, for even heaven is a constraint insofar as all will be maximally intimate with him. The former things will have passed away. This is what is "new" about the new heavens and earth (see Rev. 21:1).

Devotion and the Doctrine of God

As a result of writing this chapter and indeed this book, and of reading Origen deeply for the first time, I have come to appreciate the need to pursue teaching on God in a believing way. If our "life and conduct" (*FP* 3.1.22) is unworthy, then our thinking will not be worthy of God; our sight will be compromised. Time and time again in Origen's thought, we are reminded of how connected learning is to life and conduct. Doctrinal learning and progress is not possible without worthiness of life. Let us not embrace sin and thereby stifle learning and progress.

This chapter is a call to pursue the infinite as a mode of Christian life. God does not perfect our will "without our acts and endeavours and purpose"; our doctrine is not cleansed without our prayer and praise (*FP* 3.1.24). We must oppose, with God being our helper, the "opposing powers," Satan and his angels (*FP* 3.2.1). Without God's deliverance, however diligently we use our free will, we cannot "maintain the struggle against angels and the heights and the depth and any other creature" (*FP* 3.2.5). Participation in God's divinity is a deeply mortifying affair. The kind of training required is prayer "without ceasing" (1 Thess. 5:17), a psalmic intelligence, a heart full of evangelical zeal. Only then do we "become worthy of the grace of prophecy and of the divine gifts," worthy to unfold glimpses of God's life in ways that are not false (*FP* 3.3.3). Truthful talk about God rests on prayer; it is a function of "spiritual grace" (*FP* 3.4.3). Why? Reception of Holy Scripture's testimony to God is hamstrung without such grace. Appreciation of the "spiritual meaning" of Scripture requires spiritual readers. Spiritual readers are those with a "divine sense." They are men and women who love the one about whom they are reading. Scripture's abundant treatment of mystical and "profound matters" assumes discipline. If we are unspiritual, we will see only what "the historical narrative appears to reveal" (*FP* 3.5.1). A treatment of God's infinity, however, requires more. We need the Spirit in order to penetrate matters unseen. The spiritual meaning of the historical narrative is revealed by the Holy Spirit. Without openness to the spiritual meaning, we disregard the fact that Christian truth is both seen and unseen. To use Origen's idioms, Christian truth is a historical and spiritual matter. The spiritual meaning does not simply accompany the historical narrative but is its fulfillment. Sight fulfills knowledge; doctrine is nurtured by devotion and, ultimately, fulfilled by worship.

In becoming "spiritual people" in the Pauline sense, we become "like God," who is "the highest good" (*FP* 3.6.1; see also 1 Cor. 3:1). Christian teaching on God, indeed God's infinity, encourages likeness to God, including likeness to God's infinity. The Christian life is patterned on infinity. We are to strive to imitate and be filled by the one "who fills all in all" (Eph. 1:23), and so we acquire a kind of accidental infinity by "diligence in the imitation of God" (*FP* 3.6.1).

In many respects, we are back to the beginning of the scriptural narrative, specifically Genesis 1:26–28. Our first creation is according to the image—"in the image of God he created them; male and female he created them" (Gen. 1:27). Our end, however, is, as Origen notes, "the perfection of the *likeness*." We may in this life, "through the accomplishment of the works," fulfill in ourselves "the perfected *likeness*." Once again, our works matter. They are the means by which we attain God's likeness. Attaining God's likeness requires a disciplined program of moral and spiritual renewal. So Origen: "He might acquire it [i.e., the perfection of the *likeness*] for himself by the exercise of his own diligence in the imitation of God" (*FP* 3.6.1). Likeness to God is acquired by imitation. Image is ours at our first creation, but likeness is had by our own diligence in imitation. We are called to imitate God, and hope, in so doing, that the more we imitate, the more we see and the more are we conformed to our exemplar.

The Perennial Relevance of 1 Corinthians 15:28

First Corinthians 15:28 is important to keep considering. In the end, when Jesus comes to judge the living and the dead, and the kingdom comes in all its fullness, likeness will no longer be said of us in relation to God; likeness will give way to oneness. Origen writes that "in the consummation or end God is all in all." We must be patient here as we consider how what is finite, though possessive of a spiritual body, can be one with the infinite and bodiless God. "When all things are subjected to him"—that is, Jesus Christ—God will be "*all* in those in whom he is." Origen continues, "God is said even *to be all*" (*FP* 3.6.2). What this means for "each individual person" is that God "is all in each." What might this seemingly enigmatic phrase of Origen's mean? It means that our participation in the infinite life of the triune God will be such that God "is all in each." When there is no vice or wickedness left in us, all that we "can sense or understand or think will be all God." There will be nothing left in us that is not God. There will be an inexpressible intimacy, communion, and fellowship between God and the creature. We will no longer sense anything else apart from God; we "will think God, see God, hold God" (*FP* 3.6.3). God will be all that we are.

In terms of individuals, "God will be the mode and measure of its [i.e., each individual's] every movement, and thus *God* will be *all* to it." Our resurrected bodies will be transparent to infinity. They will be one with what God is essentially. Infinity itself "will be the mode and means" of all of our movements. God will be all to us, infinitely so. As with the angels, we will enjoy a mode of existence said to be "relatively infinite."[21] We will be one with what we have spent our lives imitating—at our best moments, anyhow. Indeed, it is not inappropriate to use the language of possession. So Origen: "All things should possess God and God should be all things to them" (*FP* 3.6.3).

Herein we see one reason that the imperishable body is so critical to Paul's argument in 1 Corinthians 15. "Those who are of heaven" will have nothing but God (1 Cor. 15:48). Because God is spirit, God cannot become conflated with what is material. "The Word became flesh" without being turned into flesh; the Word remains the Word in

21. *ST* I.7.2 (trans. Pegis, 1:58).

all that he does for us. Accordingly, the material implies limits that are inappropriate to God. Recall that God is not constrained by anything outside God—that is the point of teaching on infinity. Who we are as "imperishable" creatures will be subject to ongoing transformation. "This shall happen not suddenly, but gradually and by degrees, during the passing of infinite and immeasurable ages" (*FP* 3.6.6). Paul in 1 Corinthians 15 cannot adequately describe what will be; he cannot adequately speak of infinitely gradual conformity to the infinite God.

The sight proper to spiritual bodies will be perpetually strengthened by worship of the Lord. Ever-new splendors will be revealed. I consider it fitting, then, that what Origen calls "that other earth"— namely, heaven—is one that has "training." It may take some time for us to be rendered by the Holy Spirit "capable of God" (*FP* 3.6.9). But when we "have been rendered capable of God, then *God will be* to them [i.e., us] *all in all*." God will be all, meaning that our bodies, spiritual though they are, "will receive that highest condition to which nothing more can ever be added." The "highest condition," however, is not static. Ever-increasing glory will be "that highest condition" (*FP* 3.6.9). The more capable we are of God, the more we merit him, and the more will our manner of being resemble his. Our goal is simply to "have been rendered capable of God." That will take more than all of eternity. God's infinity is key to understanding the nature of the life of the world to come.

All of this directs us to one of the principal points of the chapter. The more one believes, the more worthily one receives "divine things" (see *FP* 4.1.7). Piety is not an add-on to a description of God's manner of being. An account of his infinity must be ever attentive to the spiritual program intrinsic to understanding infinity. Understanding is obscured by unbelief, whereas it is promoted by faith. My concern is to advance the soul, as it were, of infinity. The soul of an account of God's infinity is deeply scriptural, spiritual, and pastoral, requiring us to become the "sort of persons" we ought to be (2 Pet. 3:11).

An account of God's manner of being benefits from considering the way Paul unfolds the Old Testament mysteries. Paul does so figuratively: the "letters on stone tablets" are transformed, as are all of us, "from one degree of glory to another" (2 Cor. 3:7). The names of God have a spiritual sense. When we treat the names spiritually, we indicate "certain mystical truths" (*FP* 4.3.1). We are interweaving what we say with how we say it.[22] Of the Holy Scriptures, Origen notes that "there are inserted and interwoven things which are not accepted as history but which may hold a spiritual meaning" (*FP* 4.3.1). The names of God hold a spiritual meaning; they are relevant to the Christian life. They inform it and are its archetype. When we sing out that "the LORD is good, his steadfast love endures forever" (Ps. 100:5), we must also pray, "Teach me your statutes" (Ps. 119:68). In so doing, we become holy; we witness to God's great love. Again, the names of God, when considered in their inner meaning, provide a law "beneficial to human beings and worthy of God" (*FP* 4.3.4).

"Unveiled faces" are able to see the infinite Trinity (2 Cor. 3:18). Those who turn to the Lord have their veils removed. In this life they imitate; in the life of the world to come, they are one with the one they imitate. The Holy Spirit's ministry, therefore, does not cease with the visible manifestation of the kingdom. Indeed, the saints participate in the life of the Spirit, now in a proleptic sense, then in a way that surpasses all that we can ask or imagine. "Bodily substance is changeable," writes Origen (*FP* 4.4.6). All that God is, essentially speaking, will be ours, including God's manner of being all that he is. This will alter us to such an extent that God is *all*. Created things will, in a perfected mode of existence, receive God to such an extent that God will be all. There will be "pure and complete reception of God," ever more (*FP* 4.4.9).

What exists in God essentially is (in part) infinite goodness, love, truth, and beauty. The names of God are God's simply, perfectly. The names are one, infinitely so, with the Father, Son, and Spirit: each is infinite, not three infinities but one. Infinity is true of God, and in the next life true of us, insofar as we too will not be constrained by what is not of God. In this age, however, we struggle. We follow Christ to the cross. We acquire "through diligence and the imitation of God" not only God but inklings of God's way of being God. God has what he is infinitely. The Holy Spirit frees us in Christ to "acquire slowly and one by one" (*FP* 4.4.10) what exists forever in God.

22. Anna Williams makes this point with considerable force in *The Architecture of Theology: Structure, System, and Ratio* (Oxford: Oxford University Press, 2011).

Conclusion

I have reflected on the gains to the Christian life provided by God's infinity. First, the ministry of the Spirit is broader than the application of Christ's benefits. Though of course the Spirit unites us to Christ, taking what he has secured for us—for example, forgiveness—and sealing it on our hearts, there is more. The Spirit nurtures participation in what is God's, essentially speaking. We not only share in God's names; we obtain God's manner of being all that he is. We also share in a provisional sense, and in a face-to-face sense in the life to come, the mode in which God possesses his names. God is what he is, infinitely so. God is utterly unconstrained by what God is not. We who are spiritual are also less and less unconstrained insofar as there becomes less in us that is not of God and participant in God himself. Accordingly, the shape of Christian life is God—not only in terms of imitation but also of participation. "God is love" (1 John 4:8). The Spirit is love, and it is the Spirit that transforms us in such a way that we become God's likeness. We are "clay jars," yes, but one day we shall simply be goodness, beauty, love, all that God is, possessing heavenly bodies in the all of God, resembling God more and more, world without end (2 Cor. 4:7).

5

Immutability and the Christian Life

For I the Lord *do not change.*

—Malachi 3:6

Immutability as a divine name has profound relevance to the Christian life. We see this exemplified in Malachi 3:6–7: "For I the Lord do not change; therefore you, O children of Jacob, have not perished. Ever since the days of your ancestors you have turned aside from my statutes and have not kept them. Return to me, and I will return to you, says the Lord of hosts. But you say, 'How shall we return?'"[1] The basis for God's covenantal faithfulness is his immutability. Immutability is also the foundation for a life of repentance and trust. We shall explore this in the pages to come, beginning with the rubrics of Thomas's account.

Thomas's treatment of immutability, following as it does his account of God's existence, simplicity, perfection, goodness, and infinity, is quite straightforward.[2] Thomas begins, after citing Malachi 3:6,

1. See Thomas Aquinas, *Summa Theologiae* (hereafter *ST*) I.9.1, s.c. (trans. Pegis, 1:70). Therein Thomas cites Mal. 3:6.
2. For an extended account of divine goodness along Thomistic lines, see my book *The Lord Is Good: Seeking the God of the Psalter* (Downers Grove, IL: IVP Academic, 2018), chap. 2.

by reminding his reader of what is not the case with respect to God. There is no potentiality, no composition, and no movement in God. God "cannot acquire anything new, nor extend Himself to anything whereto He was not extended previously. Hence movement in no way belongs to Him."[3] God is in all that he causes; thus movement does not belong to him.

What is striking is the way Thomas uses the language of participation in his account of divine immutability. The more one is like God "by way of some kind of imitation," the "more fully" one "participate[s] of its likeness."[4] Taking his cues from Scriptures like James 4:8—"Draw near to God, and he will draw near to you"— Thomas notes that "God is said to approach to us, or to recede from us, when we receive the influx of His goodness or fall away from Him."[5] The more we imitate our principle, the more we participate of his goodness, and the more we can be assured that God is near to us. "Return to me, and I will return to you" (Mal. 3:7).

Not surprisingly, the preservative work of God is front and center in a robust treatment of immutability. God preserves us in being "by ever giving [us] being," says Thomas. We cannot understand our mutability apart from God; mutability is only intelligible in relation to God. "They [creatures] are mutable, inasmuch as they were producible from nothing by Him, and are by Him reducible from being to non-being." Knowledge of our mutability is a gift of God. We are created, and precisely as created we are preserved. Were God's preservative power withdrawn, we would cease to be. Thankfully, God cannot cease to be. "There is no potency to non-being" in God.[6]

At first glance, it might appear that few resources are present in Thomas's account of immutability for thinking about the Christian life. I think that such an impression is mistaken. One of the two main characteristics of our mutability is that creatures "are in potency to their end."[7] Potency in regard to our end—that is, God—means that

3. *ST* I.9.1 (trans. Pegis, 1:71).
4. *ST* I.9.1, ad. 2 (trans. Pegis, 1:71).
5. *ST* I.9.1, ad. 3 (trans. Pegis, 1:71).
6. *ST* I.9.2 (trans. Pegis, 1:73).
7. *ST* I.9.2 (trans. Pegis, 1:73). The other characteristic regards place "inasmuch as by their finite power they can attain to certain new and hitherto unattained places— which cannot be said of God."

there is in us "a mutability, through choice, from good to evil."[8] The more we choose evil, the less we are. The more we choose the good, the less we are in potency to our end. We are, therefore, less rather than more mutable. Thomas cites John of Damascus in this regard. The Damascene writes that the saints "behold God according to their capacity, and this is their food."[9] The more we choose what is God, the less potential there is in us with respect to God. We are corruptible creatures. There is in us "a potentiality to change."[10] If we continually choose evil, we cease to be. That said, the ground of our mutability remains God. "All creatures," Thomas notes, "are mutable by the power of the creator, in Whose power is their being and non-being."[11]

Choice

Choice will be a key word for us as we unfold the relationship between divine immutability and the life of faith. Not surprisingly at this point, "the good angels" provide us with a helpful initial insight. Thomas describes them as having, "besides their natural endowment of immutability of being," "also immutability of election by divine power."[12] The angels choose, without wavering, God, and they do so by divine power. Nevertheless, it is *they* who choose as they do. There is not a zero-sum game with respect to their choosing and God's power.

God does not have choice. This is one of the truths intrinsic to an account of God's immutability. However, God, who is supremely good, perfects creatures. We may follow the lead of the good angels. Like them, we may choose, by God's very own power, what is good and therefore receive "immutability of election." We also receive thereby "immutability of being." This does not imply that our being becomes our own responsibility. Rather, immutability is something that we may acquire "through choice" by divine power.[13]

8. *ST* I.9.2 (trans. Pegis, 1:73).
9. John of Damascus, *The Orthodox Faith* 2.3, cited in *ST* I.9.2 (trans. Pegis, 1:73).
10. *ST* I.9.2 (trans. Pegis, 1:73).
11. *ST* I.9.2 (trans. Pegis, 1:73).
12. *ST* I.9.2, ad. 2 (trans. Pegis, 1:73).
13. *ST* I.9.2 (trans. Pegis, 1:73).

Immutability does not in any divine sense give rise to a command-ment. Nowhere in Scripture do we find a command to "be immutable" as we do, for example, with "be perfect" (Matt. 5:48). That said, the prophetic and apostolic call to obedience is grounded in God's unwavering covenantal faithfulness. "Thus says the LORD, the God of Israel: Cursed be anyone who does not heed the words of the cov-enant, which I commanded your ancestors when I brought them out of the land of Egypt" (Jer. 11:3–4).

God's immutability—his unchangeable being—is "ethical" and "moral."[14] We discern immutability's moral character "through choice." When we who are mutable choose what is good, we glimpse our compatibility with the immutable one.[15] We were made for un-wavering intimacy with him. In choosing what is good, we increase rather than decrease in being. Our will becomes more steadfast. We become like God.

The question remains, however, as to whether we who "are under the power of sin" (Rom. 3:9) may choose what God wants to com-municate to us—namely, immutability of being and will. Choice must be situated theologically—that is, with reference to God. We remember, accordingly, what Thomas says about God as "He [who] does not preserve them in being otherwise than by ever giving them being."[16] God increases us in being by giving being. The way God gives being is by our choosing well. We thereby participate in God's immutability. As with infinity, our participation is not absolute. We are not God. "Whatever is wholly immutable can have no succession, so it has no beginning, and no end." God is eternal; God has "no beginning or end . . . [having] no succession, being simultaneously whole."[17]

Immutability is closely related to teaching on eternity. As is the case with immutability, Scripture does not call us to eternity. We do not find a commandment to "be eternal" as, again, we do with

14. Katherine Sonderegger, *Systematic Theology* (Minneapolis: Fortress, 2015), 1:3, 143. She argues that this is true with respect to all the divine names.

15. This is an instance of what I take Sonderegger to mean by "metaphysical compatibilism." Sonderegger, *Systematic Theology*, 1:82.

16. *ST* I.9.2 (trans. Pegis, 1:72).

17. *ST* I.10.1 (trans. Pegis, 1:75).

perfection. Eternity, as with immutability, is nonetheless shared with us. Thomas writes, "Nor is He eternal only, but He is His own eternity; whereas no other being is its own duration, since it is not its own being."[18] God is always "His own eternity," whereas eternal life is God's gift to us in Jesus Christ. It is proper to God, convertible with God. The same is true of immutability. We are not our own immutability; immutability is not ours. Our immutability, as with its corollary, eternity, is "participated." Neither one is proper to us. We may share in God's eternity and immutability only on the basis of God's communication of the same to us.

What is the site of God's communication of eternity and immutability? I consider choice as one of the sites wherein God communicates himself. In choosing what is right, according to Thomas, we "receive immutability from Him" and as a result "share in His eternity." The blessing we receive from choosing the good is that "of never ceasing to exist." But there is more, Thomas reminds us. We experience "unchangeableness" in being and "unchangeableness" in terms of "operation; like the angels, and the blessed, who enjoy the Word, because *as regards that vision of the Word, no changing thoughts exist in the saints*, as Augustine says."[19]

The language of choice is similar to that of "operation" in the quote above. The more we flee from "moral perversity" toward a greater "degree of disinterested devotion," the less changeable we are.[20] Although our visible bodies are subject to the ravages of death, our "inner nature is being renewed day by day" (2 Cor. 4:16) insofar as we turn toward the Lord in faith and love. The moral and spiritual health of our inner nature matters profoundly. God cannot recede from himself, but we may, however absurdly, recede from God, becoming more and more corruptible and corrupted. We often doubt, "being double-minded and unstable in every way" (James 1:8). Thus we sink "into a morass of moral degradation before the coming of our Heavenly King."[21] The more we recede

18. See *ST* I.10.2 (trans. Pegis, 1:76).
19. *ST* I.10.3 (trans. Pegis, 1:77). Thomas is citing Augustine, *Trinity* 15.16.
20. Augustine, *City of God* 1, trans. Henry Bettenson (London: Penguin, 2003), 9, 17.
21. Augustine, *City of God* 2.

from our King, the more subject we are to the adversary and thus to the ravages of change.[22]

If such is the case, then, immutability and its close corollary, eternity, have a profound moral function. Human beings that we are, we are changeable with respect to being and acts.[23] Our acts (or choices) are decisive for our being or lack thereof. Our acts of "understanding" and our "affections" determine whether we are.[24] If our morals are corrupt, we have no understanding, eventually ceasing to be. If we love the wrong things, we abscond from actuality. We pursue what lacks "permanence of being,"[25] things that "Rome" valorizes, such as "victory," "high rank," "peace" (in contrast with "felicity"), or "life" (as opposed to "eternity").[26] Let us remember that God is a far "better hope" than the gods of Rome.[27]

There is wonderful news contained in our contemplation of divine immutability. What we may say in any absolute sense of God—that God is, for example, infinite, immutable, and eternal—we may say in a relative sense of ourselves. Thus, what Thomas says of infinity is true with respect to immutability and eternity: "There is no incongruity in saying that a creature is infinite in the sense that it is not limited by any other creature."[28] What is true of God, when said of the creature, is nothing but a blessing to the creature. Just so, what is not in right relation to God destroys us. "High rank," for example, is obsessed over by Rome but is of no consequence to the heavenly city. To pursue high rank rather than holiness is to recede from being. The pursuit of high rank is a disordered pursuit, leading to nothing. When we seek after the living God, however, we receive God's infinity, immutability, and eternity. We receive these names as creatures that possess permanence of being and choice. However, we must again remember that these belong to us accidentally. Immutability is proper

22. "As eternity is the proper measure of being, so time is the proper measure of movement." *ST* I.10.4, ad. 3 (trans. Pegis, 1:79).

23. This is how human beings are different from angels. Angels have "an unchangeable being with changeableness as regards choice." *ST* I.10.5 (trans. Pegis, 1:81).

24. *ST* I.10.5 (trans. Pegis, 1:81).

25. *ST* I.10.5 (trans. Pegis, 1:81).

26. Augustine, *City of God* 2.

27. Augustine, *City of God* 2.

28. *ST* I.10.5, ad. 4 (trans. Pegis, 1:82).

to God, whereas it is ours only by participation, and participation is ours via imitation.

The Way of Life

We imitate the immutability and permanency of God by choosing what Jeremiah calls "the way of life" as opposed to "the way of death" (Jer. 21:8). The way of life is, ultimately, the way of Jesus Christ, who is "the way, and the truth, and the life" (John 14:6). Jesus Christ is the reality of the new covenant. Through the powerful working of the Spirit, Jesus Christ writes the law within us. "I will write it on their hearts" (Jer. 31:33). To the extent that the law is written on our hearts, we move toward permanency of being and choice. If God is to be ours, and we are to be God's, then God must remake us from within, inscribing his law on our hearts. When the law is written on our hearts, we are said to be infinite and immutable—that is, "not limited by any other creature."[29] Not being thus limited, we are "limited" only by God. To be limited by God, however, is to share in infinity and immutability, for God is not limited by anything. Immutability, thus understood, helps us receive the prophetic testimony of the Old Testament afresh. Time and time again, Israel is commanded to reject the gods of the nations in favor of the one true God. This Israel does not do, and so is sent into exile. But one day Israel of course will, when the law is written within. On that day Israel will be Yahweh's bride, desiring none other than him.

The command to choose the Lord assumes that we may indeed choose the Lord. The overwhelming testimony of the prophets, however, is that we do not. We (gentiles) are just like the vast majority of Israel and Judah's kings, to say nothing of the people of Israel themselves. "But your eyes and heart are only on your dishonest gain, for shedding innocent blood, and for practicing oppression and violence" (Jer. 22:17). "Moral evils," as Augustine calls them, are "the worst of evils." Fools are indifferent, Augustine argues, to "moral evils." They dread only "physical and external disasters."[30] The evils that

29. *ST* I.10.5, ad. 4 (trans. Pegis, 1:82).
30. Augustine, *City of God* 4.2.

we must not choose we do, tragically, choose. Greed, oppression, and violence—these things are so very often what we choose. When we refuse to choose the Lord, our morality is profoundly compromised. In casting aside the Lord, we open ourselves to the demons and "their disastrous effect" on morals.[31]

The divine names and the moral life are profoundly intertwined. Steadfastness is required of the people of the immutable God. The life that corresponds to the immutable God is one of single-minded hope in God. Such hope has real content. Its content is God's agency. The immutable one "is in all things, not, indeed, as part of their essence, nor as an accident, but as an agent is present to that upon which it acts." However, we are fickle creatures who rarely choose God. How then can Thomas, following Aristotle, say that "the thing moved and the mover must exist together"?[32] How can we be said to exist together with God when, like the sons of Josiah, we say, "I will not listen" (Jer. 22:21)? Even though they (and we) do not listen, "being is [nonetheless] innermost" in them as it is in us. Being itself—that is, God—is "formal" to them just as it is to us. God does not cause the apostasy of Josiah's sons, but God does cause them and us to be. The Lord God is in them as their cause—"the thing moved and the mover must exist together." Causality is the ongoing presupposition of presence. God's causality is also the presupposition for turning to God in obedience to his statutes. God is in the "children of Jacob" (Mal. 3:6), just as God is in us, insofar as God "contains" those things in which he is.[33] The Lord is in them "as an agent is present to that upon which it acts." Nothing would be without God. Though the "children of Jacob" are distant from him, they (and we) rarely listen. In refusing to listen, we are rather less like God "in nature or grace," as opposed to being more like him in terms of what we are and do.[34] The more we become like the Lord who does not change, the less distant we are from him without whom we could not be.

---

31. Augustine, *City of God* 4.2.
32. *ST* I.8.1 (trans. Pegis, 1:63).
33. *ST* I.8.1, ad. 2 (trans. Pegis, 1:64).
34. *ST* I.8.1, ad. 3 (trans. Pegis, 1:64).

True Worship

Worship of gods other than the Lord God himself is worship of demons. Augustine powerfully describes this dynamic in *The City of God*. He comments "on the harm done by the delusions of the demons, whom the Romans worshipped as gods, and their disastrous effect on Roman morality."[35] Are the demons of God? Who created them? Thomas teaches that "their nature . . . is from God" but "the deformity of sin . . . is not from Him." God is in the demons "*inasmuch as they are beings*. But in things not deformed in their nature, we must say absolutely that God is present."[36] God is not mingled in any essential sense with those spirits that hate him. Yet their existence is possible only because of God. This is a truth that they despise; they exist only because of the one they despise.

An important premise of true worship is the immutability of the one worshiped. The Lord does not change, and so we do not perish. "Return to me, and I will return to you" (Mal. 3:7). The Lord is perfect and therefore good and not subject to deformity. If we are to be like him and imitate him, living worshipfully, we must reject what deforms, opening ourselves anew to his being, power, and operation. We must cast aside the demonic. The more we are like God, the truer we are to ourselves, our very nature as human beings—"O children of Jacob" (Mal. 3:6). We abscond from the demonic. The ground of our sanctification, indeed of our return, is thus God's power, God's immediate action, touching us, as it were, "as an agent is present to that upon which it acts."[37] The more we are like God, the less remote we are from him. And the more we become like God, the less there is of us that is outside God—whereas God is also outside that which he is in. That God is in those who return to him is nothing but grace. This raises a decisive question: Is grace a more proper engine than immutability for the life of single-minded devotion?

It does not have to be an either/or, a zero-sum game. For rational creatures, "the thing desired"—God—is "in the one desiring." God is in those who seek him "as the object of operation." That we

35. Augustine, *City of God* 4.3.
36. *ST* I.8.1, ad. 4 (trans. Pegis, 1:64).
37. *ST* I.8.1 (trans. Pegis, 1:63).

possess this prerogative is "by grace."[38] The way that we are most in God is "by knowledge and will."[39] Knowing and willing are the way in which we may be said to be "in God." But it is pure grace that God is present "as the object known and loved; therefore only grace constitutes a special mode of God's existence in things."[40] That God exists in us as the one known, willed, and loved is pure grace. That God promises to "give them a heart to know that I am the LORD; and they shall be my people and I will be their God" (Jer. 24:7)—this is grace. If God is known and loved as God, then, we have before us a work of profound grace.[41] God is known and loved in grace. To know God as one who does not change and thus to become steadfast in relation to this one who does not change is entirely a work of God.

The alternative to grace, indeed to God, is the devil. The devil and the demons are a discontented lot. Those who worship them and embrace their "hubbub" are discontented too.[42] This is in stark contrast to God. One of the reasons God does not change is that God is eternally content with himself. There is nothing better than God, nothing that could make him happier than he is. God is satisfied with himself, eternally taking delight in the goodness he is. Accordingly, God's immutability is the basis of creaturely contentment. We become content only in relation to God, who not only gives happiness but also is "happiness itself."[43] God is never discontent. Those who worship him receive genuine contentment. Those who desire him who is happiness itself become happy. They forsake "exhibitions" before the gods in favor of the only one truly "worthy of his [our] worship."[44]

We thus see how the Lord's unchanging character gives rise to a rich vision of Christian contentment. Unlike the gods, who "are, in fact, demons," and "who teach depravity and rejoice in degradation,"

38. *ST* I.8.3 (trans. Pegis, 1:66).

39. *ST* I.8.3, ad. 3 (trans. Pegis, 1:67).

40. *ST* I.8.3, ad. 4 (trans. Pegis, 1:67).

41. Thomas distinguishes the mode of existence wherein God is in something by knowledge and love from his "existence in man by union." This is a reference to the incarnation of Jesus Christ, the way to union with God. See *ST* I.8.3, ad. 4 (trans. Pegis, 1:68).

42. Augustine, *City of God* 4.26.

43. Augustine, *City of God* 4.26.

44. Augustine, *City of God* 4.26.

the Lord God himself teaches satisfaction. Whereas the demons preach dissatisfaction with God, the Lord counsels tranquility. The Christian learns not to seek change for change's sake but rather to rest in relation to the one in whom she is baptized. The believer seeks things only insofar as they are related to God. Hence she forsakes the demons whose hubbub degrades and reduces one to nothing. In other words, the believer seeks containment by God. She recognizes that she cannot *be* but by God. She sees a kindred spirit in Jeremiah. "If I say, 'I will not mention him, or speak any more in his name,' then within me there is something like a burning fire shut up in my bones" (Jer. 20:9). Jeremiah must denounce his enemies, however great the cost to him personally, because their cause is groundless. His enemies will experience change for the worse: they will cease to be. They will be forgotten. Their raving is never creative, only destructive and deformative. What is unrelated to God can only degrade.

The Unchanging God

When we say that God is unchanging and consider the implications of this for the life of faith, we speak according to revelation. We move "immediately from God, by revelation."[45] We consider the divine light and the life of beatitude "through the divine light."[46] The divine light is unapproachable. "He who is the blessed and only Sovereign, the King of kings and Lord of lords. It is he alone who has immortality and dwells in unapproachable light, whom no one has ever seen or can see" (1 Tim. 6:15–16). Given that God "dwells in unapproachable light," it is appropriate to describe him in privative terms. Intellectual regeneration involves eradication of false thinking with respect to God. "For what He is not is clearer to us than what He is."[47]

The Lord who "dwells in unapproachable light" is not directly known. Scripture employs metaphors in conveyance of divine truth precisely because "divine truths are the better hidden from the unworthy."[48] In order to receive divine truth, we must become capable

45. *ST* I.1.5, ad. 2 (trans. Pegis, 1:10).
46. *ST* I.1.4 (trans. Pegis, 1:9).
47. *ST* I.1.9, ad. 3 (trans. Pegis, 1:16).
48. *ST* I.1.9, ad. 3 (trans. Pegis, 1:16).

of it. This requires moral progress. As we embrace holiness and devotion, we become worthy of receiving divine truth. God eradicates
falsity among us through obedience. Godliness and single-minded
devotion are achieved via moral progress. However, we must be set
free for holiness and devotion. The blood of Christ and the gift of
the Spirit poured out on us liberate us for a life of unwavering devotion. Consideration of God's manner of being is not an account of
the Christian life, but the latter is based on the former and, I think,
presupposes it. This book is concerned with the "moral sense" of
God as he is in himself.[49] God is our exemplar. Thus, when we say
that God does not change, we have "a type of what we ought to do."[50]

And what ought we to do? We ought not to yearn for what will
one day pass away. Accordingly, our intellects must be trained to see
temporal goods as signifying eternal goods. If we are to see rightly, we
must progress morally, seeing all that is good in a temporal sense—for
example, friendship—as pointing to and sharing in the absolute good.
"Moral progress" involves re-formed desire, the longing for gifts that
are truly important.[51] A great gift is felicity. Augustine writes of felicity, "It is an undisputed fact that felicity is the complete enjoyment of
all that is to be desired. Felicity is not a goddess, but a gift of God."[52]
Felicity is a matter of enjoying what we desire and worship. What
we desire is what the intellect sees. Just so, we see what we love, and
the more we love, the greater is our desire to see. If we see by divine
light, we see divine light. "In your light we see light" (Ps. 36:9).

Another way to say this is that we ought to will rightly. God is the
cause of all good willing, of right willing. If we do not will to be in
friendship with God, we cannot have God. However, we cannot will

49. The moral sense is language derived from Thomas's account of the threefold
division contained in Scripture's spiritual sense—namely, the allegorical, the moral,
and the analogical. See *ST* I.1.10 (trans. Pegis, 1:16–17).

50. This, again, is Thomas's language said with reference to "the New Law." So
Thomas: "Again, in the New Law, whatever our Head has done is a type of what we
ought to do." *ST* I.1.10 (trans. Pegis, 1:17).

51. Augustine, *City of God* 4.33. A gift that Augustine cites as of no importance
is one's status in this life as either a ruler or a slave. Only "his worshippers who are
still infants in respect of moral progress" yearn "for such gifts from him as if they
were of any importance."

52. Augustine, *City of God* 5, preface.

to be friends with God on our own steam. God is too great for us. The antecedent of our willing rightly is God.

Before we may proceed any further, we must consider the will's relationship to the intellect. The will is derivative of the intellect; the order here matters. The intellect is the highest part of us. After all, God is seen by the intellect, not by the senses.[53] It is our created intellect that sees the immutable God. We cannot see the immutable God, however, if we are not like God. If we will what is bad, we cannot see. Tragically, our will is all too susceptible to willing otherwise than God. When we do will to be God's by the grace of God, good things happen.

We participate in God, in whom there is no turning. God's inability to change is the antecedent for our willing a good life. A life that wills good is truly free, being subject to none other than God. When we are subject to God, in whom there is "no variation or shadow due to change" (James 1:17), we are happy.

On Not Diverging from God

When we diverge from God, the fault is ours and not God's. God can cause only what is commensurate with himself. The same is not true of us. Though we are from God, we may effect what is not of God. We may use our free will perversely. We may, and very often do, choose what is bad. Though we freely depart from the good, we cannot blame God for our devastation. God causes our will, yes, but what we do with what God causes is up to us. Augustine puts it this way: "Thus the cause which is cause only, and not effect, is God."[54] The more we are like God, the more we participate in God, and the more we do what is good.

The more we pray the prayer of our Lord, "Your will be done, on earth as it is in heaven" (Matt. 6:10), the more we are in harmony with our cause, the Lord God. The more ardently we pray this prayer, the more inviolable our "inner nature" becomes (2 Cor. 4:16). God has being in and through himself. When we pray, we become those who

53. See *ST* I.12.2 (trans. Pegis, 1:93–94).
54. Augustine, *City of God* 5.9.

gratefully receive their being in relation to God. Just as the antecedent
to our willing is God, the antecedent of our being able to pray as we
ought is God. And when we pray, we come to see "with the eyes of
[our] heart enlightened" (Eph. 1:18). The extent to which our hearts
are enlightened is the extent to which we see.[55] Grace is required, yes,
so that we may see God. Thomas calls this, in response to Psalm 36:9,
"some supernatural disposition."[56] We can see God only in relation
to God and know God only by God.

The created intellect needs God's light in order to see God's essence. But there is more. In a profound statement Thomas writes,
"By this light the blessed are made *deiform*—that is, like to God,
according to the saying: *When He shall appear we shall be like Him,
and we shall see Him as He is* [1 John 3:2]."[57] Deification has an
eschatological horizon, to be sure, but it gets at the heart of the
Christian life in the here and now. The life of faith is a matter of
ever-increasing likeness to the immutable God and Father of our Lord
Jesus Christ—God making us like to God. Deification is a matter
of becoming God, entering ever more profoundly into the life of the
triune God. The fruit of becoming like God is sight. In this life, such
sight is intellectual; it is a "glorified faculty."[58] In the life of the world
to come, we shall see God's essence with the eyes of a body rendered
immortal and spiritual.

Charity

The role of charity in relation to seeing the immutable God is important to consider. Thomas writes, "The intellect which has more of the
light of glory will see God the more perfectly. But he will have a fuller
participation of the light of glory who has more charity, because
where there is the greater charity, there is the more desire."[59] This is

55. There is a basic difference between Thomas and Augustine at this point. For
Thomas, the highest form of sight is intellectual. This is because of what grace can
do with the intellect. For Augustine, the seat of sight is the heart. I am not expert
enough in either to explain this difference.

56. *ST* I.12.5 (trans. Pegis, 1:98).

57. *ST* I.12.5 (trans. Pegis, 1:99).

58. *ST* I.12.6, ad. 3 (trans. Pegis, 1:101).

59. *ST* I.12.6 (trans. Pegis, 1:100).

a dense statement. Thomas is in part saying that the more we love God and are full of the love of God, the greater is our participation in "the light of glory." And the more we love, the more we desire the one loved. An increase in desire for God leads to increased likeness to God. God does not become more like us, but we do become more like God. Love gives rise to desire. If I "do not have love, I am nothing" (1 Cor. 13:2). When I love God, I naturally desire God, thereby becoming more like God. Love issuing in desire is, I think, the heart of the Pauline command to "be imitators of God" (Eph. 5:1).

We may therefore speak of a creaturely immutability, or of a kind of relative immutability. We as creatures are gifted with light that exceeds us. Divine light establishes us as creatures, as those who receive life solely in relation to God. God gifts us with grace rendering us capable of him. When the blessed see him, they will also see themselves in him, truly happy in their participation of him. Does this mean that our integrity as creatures is violated? No, thankfully: the immutability in which we share is accidental to us; it is subjective whereas God's is objective. An immutable existence is inaccessible to us, to be sure, but it does not contradict us. The Lord's immutability is proper to him and has no cause; immutability belongs to him of necessity. The Lord God cannot be otherwise. Remarkably, his manner of being can be participated in by us by "the light of glory," Jesus Christ.

When we see ourselves in God, we receive the gift of subjective immutability. This may be expressed as an everlasting "participation in that City on high."[60] Our participation in "that City" is immutable, without change. The days of our being tempted by what is not of the one true God will be no more. Worship will be pure, reflective of true piety. In this life, of course, our worship is not as pure as it could and should be. We must nonetheless strive to be good and to worship well. When we seek and love the one who is good, we become better, "assisted," in Thomas's words, "by the revelation of grace."[61] The Lord's revelation enables us to see him. It is the means by which he is in us. As we come to know and love him, we move, live, and see in

60. Augustine, *City of God* 5.18.
61. *ST* I.12.13 (trans. Pegis, 1:110).

relation to him. God is in the souls of the blessed, writes Thomas, "by presence, essence, and power."[62]

We must tread carefully here, for Thomas is not suggesting that God is in our soul. The preposition *by* matters. The creature, partaking of God's immutability, partakes by God's essence. As we have noted all along, God cannot be contained; God does not have being in relation to anything outside himself. And yet God is in what he causes and knows what he causes by his essence. This is why God is said to know only what is good. In knowing himself, God knows all things. What is true of him in an essential sense is the ground of his relation to creatures. God is good, and so it is fitting that God creates. Again, creatures in whom he is "by essence"—that is, creatures who are good—receive immutability in relation to him. Creatures that belong to him receive what is true of him "by presence, essence, and power." Immanence is true of his essence. Creatures blessed with immutability are assimilated to him, as it were, without being annihilated.

Friendship with God

Assimilation to God requires moral fitness. God would have us be good, unwavering in our love for him. In Augustine's words, "He it is who gives happiness in the kingdom of heaven only to the good."[63] The good are God's friends. Friendship is useful, theologically, for describing the creature's reception—as a creature—of divine immutability. "You are my friends if you do what I command you. I do not call you servants any longer, because the servant does not know what the master is doing; but I have called you friends" (John 15:14–15).[64]

---

62. *ST* I.12.11, ad. 4 (trans. Pegis, 1:108).

63. Augustine, *City of God* 5.21.

64. Fergus Kerr writes of Thomas in his pellucid piece "Charity as Friendship": "Thomas places himself between seven plausible glosses on the nature of charity, incidentally showing that thirteenth-century Catholics had a much richer range of associations than most people have today, and a set of five objections to seeing it as a kind of friendship, all of them suggested no doubt by Aristotle's *Ethics* although only two are referred explicitly to that source." In *Language, Meaning and God: Essays in Honour of Herbert McCabe, OP*, ed. Brian Davies, OP (London: Geoffrey Chapman, 1987), 4.

To be Jesus's friend is to obey him, and the gift he gives in return is eternal life. When we obey Jesus, we live in love, as he has loved us. In this way we imitate God. As creatures, we recognize that it is we who must do what he commands us. This is our duty and our joy. The blessing is belonging to God "by presence, essence, and power."[65]

We who receive immutability are not thereby devalued. God is responsible for all that is good, true, and beautiful, and we are responsible for acting obediently in relation to the good. The Lord through our obedience renders us capable of him, gifting us with immutability and thereby calling us his friends. His immutability is thus to be reciprocated; it has a creaturely analogue. When we imitate him and live in love, we "become *good*: lovable, desirable, beautiful, intrinsically valuable."[66] When we act as God's likenesses, we share in what is intrinsically—that is, by necessity—true of God. We love God in all of God's great otherness and grandeur. And God loves us as creatures, as those whose love for him is—it is hoped, increasingly— pure, without "variation or shadow due to change" (James 1:17).

Friendship as a motif helps us understand how we become likenesses of God without ceasing to be creatures. As creatures, we come to see that we have no life apart from God. We learn by grace to let God be God and ourselves creatures, for that is what God wants us to be. God does not want us to be himself but to be his imitators and likenesses. How then can friendship exist between Creator and creature, between the Lord who commands and the creature that is to obey? Friendship exists because God makes it so. We do not call Jesus our friend, but he does, remarkably, call us his friends. We are his friends, however, only if we obey, and to obey him is to love him and our neighbor in him.[67] Crucially, when we love him, we do not disappear. We do not cease to be.[68] We are not merged into him. We remain. We are blessed, in an accidental

65. *ST* I.12.11, ad. 4 (trans. Pegis, 1:108).

66. Kerr, "Charity as Friendship," 21.

67. As Thomas "re-read Aristotle's *Ethics* he found a new depth to the idea of charity as a kind of friendship. In charity we are friends with God." Kerr, "Charity as Friendship," 21.

68. "The syndrome in theology and piety that attracted Thomas's criticism over the years . . . was a certain supernaturalism that effectively devalued our humanity and our world." Kerr, "Charity as Friendship," 20.

or subjective sense, with a share in all that is common to him and his Father and their Spirit.

If such is the case, then, our partaking as creatures in God's immutability is fundamentally moral. As Rowan Williams says, teaching on the names of God "offer[s] a world to live in."[69] Our nature as creatures does not cease. Again, God loves us as creatures that he wills to transfigure. What is made new by the gospel of God is the mode in which our nature exists. We are no longer simply creatures but creatures who are called friends. Creatureliness is perfected in friendship. The principle of the noncompetitive relation between God and creatures is salient at the level of friendship. Our becoming friends of God in Jesus Christ by the power of the Spirit opens us to God's own immutable life in such a way that we are healed, not destroyed.[70]

Jesus calls us—that is, those who obey—friends. Williams raises the question of how we are to "*act* towards Jesus" and "to *speak*—*about* as well as *to* him."[71] Moreover, how are we to act toward and speak to Jesus, and to our Father, as a friend? Our being friends with God and God with us is a capacity that exceeds us, though not God. The direction is from the Trinity to us. The immutability of the triune God does not exclude God from us, mutable creatures that we are.[72] Rather, the Trinity's immutability is the ground and shape of our friendship with the Trinity. Jesus made known to the disciples everything that he heard from the Father. Such communication of course exceeded them, though it was not contrary to them. After all, Jesus chose them; the disciples did not choose him. They were created through him so as to be his disciples and, ultimately, his friends.

69. Rowan Williams, *Christ the Heart of Creation* (London: Bloomsbury, 2018), xi.

70. See Williams, *Christ the Heart of Creation*, xiii. As salutary as Williams's account is, I am not sympathetic to his language of "model"—that is, of developing a noncompetitive model of how divine and human action relate. Instead, I am seeking to describe the way of life engendered by the divine names. The language of "model" is slightly abstract in light of the moral nature of God's relation to creatures.

71. Williams, *Christ the Heart of Creation*, xvi.

72. Though Williams's discussion is about how "the infinite cannot be 'excluded' from the finite," what he says applies to the immutable in relation to the mutable. The former is capable of existing in the latter and indeed of transfiguring it.

Williams's language of "duality" is helpful in terms of under-standing this mystery. We are finite and mutable creatures. None-theless, God, by virtue of his gracious activity, configures our "fi-nite agency such that it communicates more than its own immanent content."[73] We are able to participate in the immutable life of God without ceasing to be creatures. To receive immutability is a matter of obedience perfected. Our creatureliness is able by grace to partake of and receive what exceeds it without being turned into what we receive—that is, turned into God. Stated differently, and as noted previously, God is in the blessed "by presence, essence, and power."[74] We receive from God, though God does not receive from us.

The divine names, those names common to the Three, generate not only "a new and fuller grasp of the 'grammar' of createdness" but also better understanding of the Christian life.[75] To live with immu-tability of purpose with respect to "what the master is doing" (John 15:15) does not lead to our abasement but rather to our exaltation. Yes, we are to be last, not first (Mark 9:35), decreasing in the sense pioneered by John the Baptist (John 3:30). Yet our being last is the means of our increase, our being made first. When Christ increases, we love our neighbor as ourselves and thereby increase. In so doing, we are not Christ's rivals but friends, intimate with his Father in heaven through the power of the Spirit.

Friendship with the immutable God generates piety. The kind of piety in line with the immutable God assumes worship. We worship God because he is life, unchanging and unceasing life. We worship him for his sake "and not for earthly and temporal blessings."[76] God's unchanging goodness is the ground of our worship, and it may be apprehended only in worship. One cannot be virtuous without being pious, and neither virtue nor piety is possible "without the true wor-ship of God."[77] Worship is not only the prerequisite for unfolding

73. Williams, *Christ the Heart of Creation*, 5. Though Williams is speaking in terms of the infinite/finite, we may, I think, say the same of the immutable/mutable.

74. *ST* I.12.11, ad. 4 (trans. Pegis, 1:108).

75. Williams, *Christ the Heart of Creation*, 6. Williams's concern is with how Christology generates a rich account of createdness, whereas mine is with the spiri-tual and moral grammar generated by the divine names.

76. Augustine, *City of God* 5.18.

77. Augustine, *City of God* 5.19.

the divine names but also their ongoing principle of intelligibility. The divine names, in other words, may be properly understood and received only with reference to the worshipful life.

The life of true worship assumes that the one worshiped is eternal and unchanging. The worshipful life is not desirous of things temporal but rather of the one who is immortal. Worship trains our affections in such a way that we begin to desire everlasting things. God is good, giving eternal life to those who hope for eternal life from him. God gives such life precisely because he himself is life, unchangeably and immutably. The Lord's "eternal life," as Augustine says, "is the condition of unending felicity."[78] The principle of the gospel's benefits is God, God's unending felicity. To live in fellowship with the eternal God in this mortal life is to desire God above all else. In the life to come, we shall possess and be possessed by God—what could be better than that!

Conclusion

As in the previous chapters, I have offered glimpses of God's divinity, in the case of this chapter via his immutability. I have not tried to say everything. Instead, I have sought to sketch truth intrinsic to the Trinity's immutability. What is more, I have not simply described immutability. I have, to use Augustine's remarkable language, not only gestured toward what is true of divinity but also attempted to show that "the true and holy Divinity is to be sought and worshipped . . . for the sake of the life of blessedness."[79] My concern is not simply with the names convertible with the divine being itself. Rather more is at hand—namely, to present those names as names to be *sought* for "the life of blessedness." This book is preoccupied not only with seeking the truth but also with the true God as the one who must be worshipped.

The life of blessedness is a sharing in God, indeed a sharing, as creatures, in God's immutable manner of being God. Such sharing takes in this life the form of imitation. God is rich in his immutability,

78. Augustine, *City of God* 6.12.
79. Augustine, *City of God* 7, preface.

as is the case with riches of his infinity, perfection, simplicity, and existence. And the blessing of the gospel is that he makes us rich in him—"For [our] sakes he became poor" (2 Cor. 8:9). The Lord Jesus delivers us from superstition and the demonic, enabling us to worship him and his Father in their Spirit, the one "living, incorporeal, unchangeable" God.[80] In the next chapter, we consider a particular dimension of christological teaching, the hypostatic union, the union of divinity and humanity in the person of God the Son. In thinking about the union, we deepen our understanding of divinity as that which may be apprehended only in seeking and imitation.

---

80. Augustine, *City of God* 7.19.

Part Two

6

The Hypostatic Union
and the Christian Life

*And all of us, with unveiled faces, seeing the glory of the
Lord as though reflected in a mirror, are being transformed
into the same image from one degree of glory to another.*

—2 Corinthians 3:18

In this chapter we consider a facet of christological teaching that
helps us clarify how we as creatures receive what is proper to our
Creator without our ceasing to be creatures. Rowan Williams will
be our main contemporary interlocutor, with Augustine the mainstay
from the tradition.

The relationship between what is finite and infinite "can never,"
Williams argues in *Christ the Heart of Creation*, "be one in which
more of one means less of the other."[1] He is echoing the likes of
Kathryn Tanner on this point.[2] God and creatures "are not in rivalry"

---

1. Rowan Williams, *Christ the Heart of Creation* (London: Bloomsbury, 2018), 11.
Hereafter *CHC* and cited in the text. Though Williams's discussion is with respect
to "agency," the same may, I think, be said of "being."
2. See, e.g., Kathryn Tanner, *Christ the Key* (Cambridge: Cambridge University
Press, 2010), chap. 1.

(*CHC*, 12). When we receive a participation in God's divinity, however subjective, relative, and accidental it may be, we must remember that God is not one who operates "in the same mode, the same metaphysical territory" as we do (*CHC*, 21). "God is God," as Karl Barth was fond of saying. God creates us in such a way that we are capable of more than we are. God creates us for himself.

How may we gain insight into this remarkable truth regarding creaturely participation in God? We look toward the humanity of Jesus. To see the man Jesus as he is involves seeing him as the Word, the Father's eternally beloved Son, on whom the Spirit rests. This man, Mary's son, is "inseparable from the eternal *esse* of the Word" (*CHC*, 33). This is of course not true of us: we are not the Word; we are rather born of the Word and Spirit in accord with the will of the Father. As we come to worship in spirit and in truth, we learn that our being is not our own. We discern that we belong to the Word. However, our *esse* is not that of the man Jesus: his *esse* is the Word. He is the Word. His humanity, in turn, is fundamentally receptive; he eternally receives himself from the Father. This truth has profound implications for how we think about Jesus's humanity. His humanity, Williams explains, "contributes nothing extra to that identifying *esse*." This is very technical. And yet a simple point is being made—namely, the eternal Word is "the activating principle of the life of Jesus" (*CHC*, 35). Jesus does not make the Word, whereas the Word makes him. You cannot truthfully describe who Jesus is without describing him as the Word, the eternal Son of the Father.

This basic point should inform how we think about our reception of and sharing in the divine life. We are finite and mutable creatures, yes, but we receive from God in a manner analogous to how the man Jesus receives from the Word. "Genuine finite substantiality" is said of us as it is said of the man Jesus. In Jesus's case, this is said of him in a way that maintains "the immutability of the divine Person." Jesus is the Word, and he shall never cease to be the Word. In order to say this, as we must, we need a certain kind of "conceptual structure" (*CHC*, 37). Here Williams, following Thomas, is especially helpful. The key notion is *esse*. There is "unity of *esse*" between Jesus and the Word (*CHC*, 40). Divinity and humanity do not compete with each other in him. As we shall see, the same is true of us in fellowship with God. There is unity between humanity and God in Jesus Christ. We learn in Jesus Christ to no longer compete with God but to be God's friends.

The parallel in terms of our sharing in God via imitation is as follows. Although there is—of course!—not "unity of *esse*" between the believer and Jesus, there is unity, a great intimacy, though not between equals. Jesus is the Savior. When we take up our cross, deny ourselves, and follow him, we affirm that there is unity between him and us. The Christian, however clumsily, learns via the mortification and vivification of her flesh that she has no other "activating principle" than Jesus and the Spirit (*CHC*, 36). The Christian, as with the man Jesus, is "inseparable from the eternal *esse* of the Word" (*CHC*, 30). But unlike the man Jesus, the Christian's inseparability is not eternal in nature. There was a time when the world was not. But even then, the man Jesus subsisted in the Word who in the "fullness of time" became flesh (Gal. 4:4). Yes, we are inseparable from Jesus insofar as we learn to say with Paul that "it is no longer I who live, but it is Christ who lives in me" (Gal. 2:20). That inseparability is not substantial but accidental—true by reference to his grace. The inseparability of the believer with respect to Christ is Christ's work. He died for us. The union of the believer with Christ is what Christ achieves for us—I once was lost but now am found. Having said that, we through Christ and in the Spirit become capable of God, not simply in terms of imitation of God but also in terms of participation. We receive from Jesus the perfect, infinite, and immutable life common to him, the Father, and the Spirit without ceasing to be creatures. God's life in Christ transfigures us; it does not destroy us. If such is the case, then, the hypostatic union illuminates the Christian life. The union helps us understand the dynamics of our sharing in what is God's. Our lives are "hidden with Christ in God" (Col. 3:3).

This leads us to the place where we may think with some clarity about our being in Christ. The believer in Jesus shares in his filial relationship with the Father. We are adopted children of the Father in Jesus Christ and in the Spirit. In defining us through our baptism, the Lord Jesus opens us in his Spirit "to his agency and [to] growing into a different kind of existence as a result of that agency . . . in the sense that what they [believers] do and say in the name or *persona* of

Jesus counts as done or said by Jesus" (*CHC*, 55). That is important to think about, but it is not enough. Jesus defines us, yes, and thus opens us to his agency. Even more, he shares his very being with us, common to him, the Father, and the Spirit. The benefits of the gospel—think, for example, of the forgiveness of sins—communicate the divinity we receive from them. The missions of Son and Spirit, and the works those missions accomplish, transfigure us. God "has shone in our hearts to give the light of the knowledge of the glory of God in the face of Jesus Christ" (2 Cor. 4:6). Receptivity to divine action indicates receptivity to divine being. Openness to God's action is coincident with reception of the divine nature (*CHC*, 56).

Believing Agency and Being

Close study of the hypostatic union deepens understanding of the relation between the believer's being as well as agency and God's. Jesus's "divine nature or agency is [not] a vastly magnified version of finite agency" (*CHC*, 63). The Lord is unequivocally and absolutely divine. God's works of grace and the benefits they communicate—chiefly, participation in the divine life—do not then simply better or perfect us. Though this is true, they accomplish something more radical, "new creation" (2 Cor. 5:17). Jesus Christ renders us capable of what thoroughly exceeds us, the perfect, infinite, and immutable life of the I AM, the Lord himself. The contrast, then, with Jesus Christ is instructive. Unlike us, he does not need to be rendered capable of divine existence. Jesus's humanity is always the humanity of the Logos. Jesus grows in "wisdom," to be sure, and learns understanding through what he suffers, but he does not grow into being God's beloved Son (Luke 2:52). He *is* God's Son. Sin is original to us, and the gift of God in Jesus Christ makes us into that which we were not before, God's adopted children as opposed to "children of the devil," following 1 John 3:10.

Even as we are born of God in Jesus Christ through the Spirit, we do not cease to be creatures. Insofar as we imitate God and live in love, God works in us, intensifying our capacities in such a way that we are rendered capable of him. The difference with Jesus Christ is stark. Again, the man Jesus learns, grows, and suffers as one unequivocally human, but his humanity is unequivocally that of the Word. We, however, have our humanity only through the Word. Jesus says what he says and does what he does because of the Word. Jesus is human in the way that he is because of the Word. The man Jesus, notes Williams, following Augustine, "becomes wholly a vehicle of *communication* for the divine Word" (*CHC*, 71). Our relation to the Word ought to be like that of Jesus's, fundamentally receptive. We, like Jesus in all his unequivocal humanity, receive, but unlike him we in receiving enjoy a new relation to God. Jesus, however, enjoys no new relation to the Father. The being of his person does not change. As "a voice from heaven said, 'This is my Son, the Beloved, with whom I am well pleased'" (Matt. 3:17).

Here we see how the Christian is both similar to and different from Jesus Christ. When we talk about the Christian's identity, we must point to Jesus Christ. The Christian lives because of him. She is, like Jesus of Nazareth himself, a "composite" reality.[3] But again, we must proceed very carefully. To say "composite" with respect to Jesus is to say "Jesus of Nazareth as animated and actualized by the Word" (*CHC*, 89). To say "composite" with respect to the Christian is to say that the Christian is animated and actualized by Jesus Christ and his Spirit. Of course, the dissimilarities are immediately evident. I, unlike Jesus Christ, frequently grieve his Spirit, whereas Jesus neither grieves his Father nor their Spirit. And yet I, like Christ, am animated and actualized by "another" (I use this word loosely). If I am to confess Jesus Christ aright, I must confess him in relation to the Word; if I am to describe the Christian person aright, I must describe her in relation to Christ. The dissimilarity between the Christian and Christ is thus immediately apparent. Jesus is the incarnate Word. The Word is an eternal reality, eternally born of the Father. Jesus's "created agency is real and distinct," and yet it contributes nothing to "what the Word eternally is by definition" (*CHC*, 90). Jesus's action does not make him into who he is: his divinity (his *esse*) is not a project. Just as Jesus does not make the Word in any sense to be the Word, so we (Christians) are not the agents of our rebirth and transformation.

---

3. This is Thomas's language, language that Williams endorses and appropriates. See, e.g., *CHC*, 89.

Jesus is. Our integrity and unity as Christian individuals resides in the Word. The principle of unity of Jesus's humanity, similarly, resides in the Word. Jesus's unity with the Word, however, is essential, whereas we are united with him by grace, subject in this life to the mortifying and vivifying work of the Spirit.

The believer, as is the case with the humanity of Jesus Christ, exists only in relation to the Word. The Word constitutes the humanity of Jesus, similarly the believer. That said, the believer is not identical to Jesus Christ, though Jesus Christ is identical to the Word. There is a real difference here. The Word's assumption of humanity in Jesus provides an important context for thinking about how the finite shares in and receives God's manner of being without thereby ceasing to be creaturely. We recall a truth fundamental to Christian faith. We are not God; we are not the Word himself, who is entirely identical to the divine life. And yet the Word himself raises us to not only "a new level of agency" but also a new level of being without our "basic structure being changed" (*CHC*, 101). What do we mean by our "basic structure" remaining intact? Going beyond Williams's account, I think that we must talk on the level of activity and of being. Glorified humanity is perfectly receptive of God. Whether in this life or in the life to come, we exist only in relation to God. We are and always will be creatures. But as glorified creatures in heaven, our being will be divine. We as creatures will be utterly activated by the being of God. The humanity of Jesus provides the pattern for heaven. Jesus does not cease to be truly human because the Word activates him. Similarly, we will not cease in heaven to be creatures, but we will be creatures capable of a profoundly heightened level of being—an "optimal actuality," to use Williams's language (*CHC*, 104). We are talking about not only intensification of agency but also intensification of being. With Williams we do want to say that our human nature "is oriented towards realizing in the finite world the character or quality of the infinite reality which is the Word's loving dependence on the Father." But more than that, the divine names indicate the infinite reality in which we come to share. To be a baptized child of God is to share in not only "the operation of the divine nature" but also something of that nature itself "without ceasing to be created" (*CHC*, 105). As Williams says of Maximus, our vocation "is the realization in humanity of a divine mode or style of existing" (*CHC*, 108). As we have seen, God's existence, manner of existence, perfection, infinity, and immutability—understood as names—show us the "style of existing" that is our vocation. It is Jesus who in the Spirit enables us to live as he does—that is, in a filial way—and to be as he is.

Our lives as believers involve a process. The Lord Jesus, through the church's preaching and the celebration of her sacraments, renders us his friends. He not only defines us but also shares what he is, Godhead itself. Our existence is patterned after Christ's cross. As we follow and love him, we receive the Spirit with which we are baptized, acquiring "a life *huper phusin*, beyond our given capacities" (*CHC*, 121). We become children of God, recipients of and sharers in the life common to the Father, Son, and Spirit. The hypostatic union (again) helps us understand this. Just as the humanity of Jesus is informed and completely defined by the Word, so too is the Christian defined by what "is real at a completely different ontological level" (*CHC*, 121). But there is more: we are not simply defined by God but sustained by God in such a way that we imitate God and live in love. And again, that life we receive as we imitate him has a cruciform shape. He gives us the capacity to die—to die to all that is incommensurate with his kingdom.

The spiritual life is a matter of imitating God, which is to live like the man Jesus Christ. Just so, the spiritual life involves our actions but also our being remade as we follow Jesus to the cross, dying daily. "I die every day!" (1 Cor. 15:31). We are made for God and to receive God in light of the kind of creatures we are. As we saw, the hypostatic union reminds us that Jesus's humanity does not exist in a competitive relationship with the eternal Word. The man Jesus is ceaselessly receptive of the eternal Word as one hypostatically united to that same Word. This is not true of us: we are not the Word. But to the extent that we follow the Word, we receive the life of the Word, denying ourselves and following him. We receive a kind of limitlessness as creatures—a kind of relative infinity, if you will—in the life to come. What we are and what we do—both shall become wholly and unqualifiedly animated by God and God's Spirit. In this life, we live in light of the future. We strive toward ever-greater continuity between

God and ourselves, not only on the level of agency, but in terms of being, thereby working out our salvation in fear and trembling.

Consideration of the divine names is therefore a spiritually charged undertaking. God desires that there be continuity between himself and creatures. God wants us to act and be in a way that is of him. Therefore it is important to talk about how the truths of God's manner of being shape our lives before God. God creates us as those who are infinitely open to his being, walking, as it were, with him in the garden. As we look to God's beloved Son, Jesus Christ, we see that a human life identical with the eternal Word is maximally human. This is, of course, not a life fused with or collapsed into the Word. The Word exists humanly. We too are called to exist humanly, to respond to Christ's call, and to follow him to death; we become ourselves as Jesus Christ radically heals us. Accordingly, God's being is not added to our being. Our creaturely being is expanded, intensified, and deepened in such a way that we see, know, and experience ourselves and everything else in relation to God. Hence the function of teaching on the hypostatic union: it encourages us to appreciate how we may be said to be recipients of God's being and manner of being. In receiving him, we undergo a significant expansion of ourselves.

The Great Difference

Consideration of the hypostatic union also helps us see the great difference between the Word and ourselves. The goodness of the Word, as is the case with the goodness of the Son and Spirit, is actual, whereas any goodness said of us participates in his goodness. For example, the life that the dead Lazarus receives is Jesus's life. Through the Spirit, the Lord Jesus gives to Lazarus the life he is. What is Jesus's by nature becomes Lazarus's by grace. Lazarus is not obliterated but rather raised up.

When we are united with the person of the Word, we are united to all that he has in common with the Father and Spirit. The language of participation works on an essential level. What is said of one person—for example, that the Son is born—is not to be said of their one essence. Talk of the Word's begottenness is personal. The life of the Word is the perfect, infinite, and immutable life of God,

Father, Son, and Spirit. In being united to the Word, we are united to his being, uncreated life, life that is compatible with us. He makes us new, taking away what is incompatible with him. Nothing remains in the way of our receiving him as he is. This is true not only in terms of what he is but also in terms of what he does.[4]

This means that when we look in faith to Jesus, we see the only "place in the finite world where relation with the divine action is unimpeded" (*CHC*, 155). When we imitate him, not only is divine action less and less impeded in us, but so is divine being. We are transfigured in terms of both what we do and what we are. This does not denote the abolition of the human, indeed of creatures, as finite. It indicates, rather, new creation. New creation is more a matter of the radical indwelling of God in what is absolutely different from God. On the level of action, "it is no longer I who live, but it is Christ who lives in me" (Gal. 2:20); on the level of being, I receive what utterly exceeds me. There is thus "unconditioned freedom of engagement" on the level of being and activity (*CHC*, 165). God delights in us, for there is less and less in us that is not of him. Consequently, we have no delight other than God, and we delight in other things only in relation to God.

Christian life is a matter of openness to God, to the life of the crucified and resurrected Jesus who breathes out his Spirit among us. This is our vocation, to be open to the gift of God in Jesus Christ. As we open ourselves to him, our createdness is not displaced. We become more rather than less human. God's work in the incarnate Word, Jesus Christ, is, as Williams notes, "directed toward the wholesale pervading of created reality by the divine without any loss of its integrity" (*CHC*, 170). More specifically, the life of the Christian is pervaded—more and more, so it is hoped—by divine activity and divine being. This is, to be sure, Christian life, but as such it is also human life. To be a creature is to live in a fundamentally receptive relation to God. Just as the Word receives nothing, ontologically speaking, from the humanity of Jesus—Jesus does not make the Word

4. Once again, my account differs somewhat from Williams's. In terms of the hypostatic union, Williams is interested in disentangling finite and infinite agency. My interest is in questions not only of agency but also of being—that is, disentangling finite and infinite being.

the Word—so too are we (and not God) enriched by living lives of receptive praise. We are united in the waters of baptism to the Word, and in him to the person of the Father, and all that through the person of their Spirit. Just so, we are united to their essence, receiving a share in their manner of being. We share, that is, in a "recognizably human" way in what is God's (*CHC*, 180).

The incarnation teaches us that the life of God is expressible "in the entirety of a human life, so that human nature [the human nature of the one person of the Word] comes to be expressed in terms of God's life" (*CHC*, 196). The Son of God is capable of existing humanly, even of dying the most ignominious death imaginable. His humanity is at all points expressive of God's life. The parallel with the Christian is clear. The Christian, by virtue of the powerful working of grace, is also to be a person whose humanity "comes to be expressed in terms of God's life" (*CHC*, 196). We are not our own. The asymmetry between God and us is also clear. It is God expressing his life in and through us, not us expressing our life—which is, of course, not our own—through him. We are not capable of existing divinely. But the Son of God is capable of existing humanly. The gift of his justification and sanctification in the Spirit is that he makes us capable of existing divinely, of living in a holy way amid the wreckage of our postlapsarian condition. What is more, in existing divinely we fulfill our vocation as humans. The great I AM declares himself through us and indeed through all things insofar as they are related to him.

The Christian is intelligible only in relation to God. Where are you from? Whose are you? What Hosea says to an exiled people is also said to us: "Your faithfulness comes from me" (Hos. 14:8). All that is praiseworthy in you is of me, says the Lord God. You are mine. You are from me insofar as you worship me and live prayerfully in relation to me. I cause you and desire to see and know myself in you. The Christian, echoing Paul, thus says, "Now I know only in part; then I will know fully, even as I have been fully known" (1 Cor. 13:12). Contemplation of God's being and manner of being is important precisely because God causes in us what is of himself. God is not incompatible with creatures. Accordingly, we seek to live not merely a life that is correspondent with God but one that God sees and knows. This is a dependent life, yes, but even more it is a life anchored in love.

To be a lover of God—this is our vocation. Hear Augustine's match-less words: "Always acting as God," God is "present everywhere in his totality, free from all spatial confinement, completely untrammelled, absolutely indivisible, utterly unchangeable, and filling heaven and earth with his ubiquitous power which is independent of anything in the natural order. He directs the whole of his creation, while allow-ing to his creatures the freedom to initiate and accomplish activities which are their own; for although their being completely depends on him, they have a certain independence."[5]

The Lord delights in our being creatures who, because they love him, enjoy him and "have a certain independence." Our joy and duty in this mortal life is to love him who is "untrammelled," "indivis-ible," and "unchangeable." Our happiness lies in enjoying this one we are learning to love, receiving from him, subjectively speaking, an existence that is "untrammelled," "indivisible," and "unchange-able." Again, in Augustine's words, "He who has set his heart on God will be happy in the enjoyment of him."[6] We shall in heaven enjoy an untrammelled, indivisible, and unchangeable relationship with our God and Father. Let us live now in such a way that we gesture toward what shall be. Until heaven comes down to earth, we strive to love the Trinity.

Superiority to the Demonic

When we love God, our superiority to the demons is manifest. A life that loves God is a life, notes Augustine, "of goodness and integrity." Specifically, Augustine highlights "moral goodness" as that "which gives us pre-eminence over the demons."[7] A life that is morally good is a life rightly ordered to God. A morally good life resembles God; such a person is an imitator of God, living in love. Although our bodies are wasting away, our soul may remain superior to the demons insofar as we subject ourselves to God. In subjecting ourselves to God—which is the way of "the true religion"—we are set "free from the vicious

5. Augustine, *The City of God* 7.30, trans. Henry Bettenson (London: Penguin, 2003), 292.

6. Augustine, *City of God* 8.8.

7. Augustine, *City of God* 8.15.

tendencies in which we resemble them [the demons]!"[8] The demons are vicious because they do not love God, and they are miserable because they do not enjoy their worship of themselves. The worshipful soul does not fear them, precisely because in life and in death she fears God. She worships God and models herself on Jesus Christ. True religion is, as Augustine notes, a matter of modeling "oneself on the object of one's worship."[9] The demons are not worthy of our worship, and so worship of them is madness, whereas there is none more worthy of worship than the Lord God himself. To obtain moral goodness is to model oneself on him. Those who are good in a moral sense naturally worship God, demonstrating how compatible are "the essential divine attributes and the living of a recognizably human life" (CHC, 180). The God we worship is imitable. It is possible for us to be good, just as God is good, though of course God's goodness is uncreated. It is possible for us to be created analogues of his existence, manner of existence, perfection, infinity, and immutability.

Worship of the triune God is humanizing. The demons are as vicious as they are because they have pretensions to divinity. They hate God. The demons work tirelessly so as to prove to us that they—and not Israel's God—are divine and therefore worthy of worship. The demons have, however, failed even at that. And so, as Augustine argues, they pretend that "they are intermediaries between gods and men, securing for mankind the benefits of the gods."[10] The demons know how susceptible we are to worshiping golden calves, and so they encourage such worship so as to draw us into intimacy with themselves. Hence the perennial relevance of Jesus's temptations: Jesus is faithful where his people were not faithful. He lives on God's word alone, refuses to test God, and serves only him (see Matt. 4:1–11). He shows himself to be God's Son, expressing the "divine life in the entirety of a human life" (CHC, 184). Jesus is therefore triumphant over the devil and experiences the angels waiting on him.

We must not befriend false gods, for in so doing we shall become as they are, mischievous and vicious. Rather, we must worship, imitate, and model the one true God who fills "heaven and earth with his

8. Augustine, *City of God* 8.17.
9. Augustine, *City of God* 8.17.
10. Augustine, *City of God* 8.22.

ubiquitous power." Thus, God allows his creatures "the freedom to initiate and accomplish activities which are their own" (*CHC*, 292). We are given the freedom and the power to witness in the Spirit to Jesus Christ. We are thereby delivered from trying to copy him or, worse, to make him "relevant." Instead, we are to live as he does— that is, in humble submission to his Father and in obedience to his will. Though Christians know that "the whole cosmos rests entirely upon the wicked one," Christians also know that they are "of God" (1 John 5:19 DBH). The Christian person "keeps watch" over herself, avoiding sin, and therefore whatever is of the idols (1 John 5:18 DBH).

We need the support and instruction of the Lord Jesus Christ and his angels. At key points in the Gospel narratives, the angels are present to Christ, ministering to him. It is a sign of his humility that he through whom the angels were made receives help from them. Just as Christ received their ministry, so too do we, though we may not always recognize it. In becoming like Christ, we resemble the angels. We acquire a taste for heavenly things.

It is important to think about the angels because in becoming united to God in Christ and the Spirit, we resemble the angels. "When we are restored to health and so become like the angels," notes Augustine, "we come near to them even now by faith."[11] Just as we come near to Christ by believing in him, so too do we become intimate with his angels by believing. When we open ourselves to the life of God, we open ourselves to his angels. The angels do not make us happy; only God does. However, they support us in being happy in God, and God supports their ministry of encouraging his happiness in us.[12] We resemble what we worship, and the more we worship the Trinity, the more we resemble the angels and the more we enjoy their help. When the kingdom is consummated, we shall cease being inferior to the angels, sharing not only "rationality" with them—as we do now—but also immortality.[13]

Our share in immortality is only possible because of Jesus Christ, "the good mediator." How so? Because the incarnate Word does not become the Word but is eternally the Word of the Father. He "was

---

11. Augustine, *City of God* 8.25.
12. See further Augustine, *City of God* 8.25.
13. Augustine, *City of God* 9.13.

willing to be mortal for a time."[14] His equality with the Father and
Spirit never diminishes. He is able to save those who call out to him
and bless them with angelic support. That the Word is able to save
as he does, to come among us in the man Jesus to consummate the
promises made to his people, rests on one foundational truth: his
Godhead. Not only the hypostatic union but also his works and the
benefits that follow are possible because of his Godhead. Because
of the Word, the multitude is "made blessed by participation in the
one God."[15] We are blessed by participation in God's being and manner of being through the person of the Mediator. He binds us to
himself in his Spirit and keeps us in relation to himself through the
sacramental ministry of the church, blessing us with the riches of the
consubstantial Trinity.

We participate in God's nature—a nature common to the Three—
through the Son and in the Spirit. When we talk about God's nature,
we are talking on a substantial level, and when we discuss the personal, we note how the nature or essence common to the Three is
uniquely possessed by each of them. Christ communicates his life
to us in the Spirit. By participating in him by faith, we, as Augustine
states, "reach our felicity . . . the uncreated Word of God, by whom
all things were created." When we participate in him who partakes
of all that we are (save sin), we receive "a short cut to participation
in his own divine nature." And of course participation "in his own
divine nature" is participation in the blessed Trinity, "in which the
angels participate, and so achieve their felicity."[16]

Another way to say this is that substantial participation has, in
this life, a personal form. Again, in an unforgettable turn of phrase,
Augustine says of Christ that "in the lower world he was the Way of
life, and in the world above he is the Life itself."[17] Christ is the way
to the Father, and the way to substantial participation in the very
life that he mediates.

We do not enhance Jesus's divinity; we do not contribute to him in
any way. One of the two greatest truths of the incarnation, Augustine

14. Augustine, *City of God* 9.15.
15. Augustine, *City of God* 9.15.
16. Augustine, *City of God* 9.15.
17. Augustine, *City of God* 9.15.

argues, is "that the true divine nature cannot be polluted by the flesh, and that demons are not to be reckoned our superiors because they are not creatures of the flesh."[18] The former is easier for us to accept on some level anyhow, the latter more difficult. We do not have any kind of (polluting) impact on God—so far so good. But the inferiority of the demons is more difficult for us to think about. They are inferior because in their knowledge they lack love. Our problem is not our corporeality—we must not think that it is so! And the demons' problem is not their lack of corporeality. Rather, the demons are inferior because they do not worship the one they know to be true. Their reason for being is entirely negative. They know who Jesus Christ is, and work as they do to discourage any "spiritual progress" in relation to him.[19]

Why mention the demons at this juncture? I mention them because they illustrate how problematic is knowledge without love. "Knowledge puffs up, but love builds up," writes Paul. "Anyone who claims to know something does not yet have the necessary knowledge; but anyone who loves God is known by him" (1 Cor. 8:1–3). The demons have knowledge but not "necessary knowledge." The believer, by contrast, has "necessary knowledge," this because charity informs her knowledge. Augustine makes this point with alarming clarity: "There is in the demons knowledge without charity, and so they are inflated."[20]

The demons occasion further insight into the hypostatic union and our reception of God. The Lord Jesus, the incarnate Word, does not evolve. The enfleshed Word never becomes more than he has always been, the eternal Word of the Father. His journey to the cross is, to be sure, perfecting, but that perfecting is in terms of his humanity. The man Jesus "learned obedience through what he suffered" (Heb. 5:8). Jesus, in the midst of unconscionable suffering, loves the Father and pours out his Spirit. His ministry is predicated on not simply knowledge of the Father but love of him, and the love he has for the Father and the Father for him is the Spirit. When we receive Jesus Christ, we are said to receive not simply one known but also one who is loved, who is love, and who pours out on us the love that is

18. Augustine, *City of God* 9.17.
19. Augustine, *City of God* 9.18.
20. Augustine, *City of God* 9.20.

his Spirit. When we receive Christ, we also resemble the angels—and not the demons!—because we "enjoy participation in his eternity."[21] The demons know God but do not love God, and so they cannot be sanctified. Therefore they are miserable. They work hard to drag us who are corporeal into their incorporeal misery and ugliness.

The beauty of Jesus Christ, which is the very beauty of God, is not something to which he clings; he is not stingy. His beauty, as with the beauty of Father and Spirit, "is not only immaterial, but immutable also and ineffable, and it enflames them [the saints] with a holy love." Jesus Christ's beauty is immaterial in the sense that it may only be seen in the Spirit. He appears to us as one lowly and despised, there being nothing in his form that commends his origin as the Father's eternally beloved. In order to see him as he is, as one who is from God, we must do good.[22] Only then will we see his visible form as revelatory of the greatest beauty and so be enflamed, as Augustine notes, "with a holy love." The Lord Jesus is generous with his beauty, beatifying us who seek and love him.

The doctrine of the hypostatic union reminds us, in part, that he is so secure in his being as the Father's beloved that he can and does share his very being, his inestimable beauty, with us in and by the power of his Spirit. Just as the Lord Jesus, together with the Father and the Spirit, renders the angels blessed, he renders us blessed, communicating to us in the gospel his life. We participate accordingly in his life (and thus the life of the Father and Spirit) and thereby receive his beauty. We worship him who always bears his wounds, glorified though he is. This is our "never-failing joy."[23] God grants us through the poverty of his Son his happiness in the Spirit, "granting them a share in his own being." In "the fullness of time," God's beloved Son assumes "the likeness of sinful flesh" in order to share with us what he is (Gal. 4:4; Rom. 8:3). We receive from him fullness upon fullness. We not only receive "adoption as his children" (Eph. 1:5) but "a share in his own being."[24]

---

21. Augustine, *City of God* 9.21.
22. Cf. 3 John 11: "Beloved, do not imitate what is evil but imitate what is good. Whoever does good is from God; whoever does evil has not seen God."
23. Augustine, *City of God* 9.22.
24. Augustine, *City of God* 9.23.

Living the Divine Life

The Christian life is thus a life of imitation, the imitation of Jesus Christ. We are to live "the divine life in the mode of reception and response" (*CHC*, 220). Insofar as we receive and imitate that life, we participate. The Christian receives the Lord and responds to him, it is hoped, and in all that she does. Though her action is not "strictly 'coincident'" with "divine action" as is the case with Jesus, her actions, as she grows in faith, become at least approximately coincident with his. Accordingly, Williams notes, "We are steered towards a similar model of relation between Creator and creation" (*CHC*, 221). As the Son is in Father, so too is the creation in an analogical sense in the Creator. Jesus is one with the Father; similarly, the creation exists in God without ceasing to be created.

As helpful as Williams's account is, it falls short. The Father-Son relation becomes a model for the Creator-creation relationship. While there are of course analogues—the Son is from the Father, and not the Father from the Son, just as the created order is from the Creator and not the reverse—I wonder whether Williams adequately honors the very great difference between Creator and creation. While Williams is drawing on Erich Przywara, who is acutely aware of the "always greater difference" within similarity of Creator and creation, I wonder whether the Father-Son relation is useful as a model for describing finite creatures' participation in the divine names. For Williams, "Jesus embodies the maximal and optimal relation of creature to Creator" (*CHC*, 226). That is of course true. But I think that there is more, insofar as the divine names help us see how the infinite God transfigures the finite, granting it a participation in himself. Our acts, as with our being, are analogically related to God. My concern is with describing how our being (and not simply our acts) is "understood in terms of greater or less alignment with the infinite movement of God to God" (*CHC*, 226). Not just our acts but our very being is to imitate God, and so to enjoy a degree of participation in him.

Jesus Christ, in and by the power of the Spirit, proclaims the rule of God; in so doing he proclaims himself the subject and agent of the kingdom. He calls us to follow him and to conform to his rule. Jesus Christ, the incarnate Word, not only shows us but brings about in us true creatureliness. The Christian life is enriched, profoundly, by the classical doctrine of the incarnation, as it is by the doctrine of creation's contribution to the Creator-creature distinction. The divine names have important theological work to do in helping us see how we participate in the names common to the one essence. The divine names help us see how our participation in God takes the shape, in this life, of imitation.

The hypostatic union teaches us that the finite and infinite perfectly coincide in the man Jesus. Williams puts it this way: the incarnation affirms "the transforming *coincidence* of the finite and infinite in the detail of this finite life" (*CHC*, 236). But there is more. What gets shortchanged, I think, is the revelatory power of the Book of Nature. What God is "is revealed in Christ," yes, but not only in Christ (*CHC*, 234). Christian life is beholden to Jesus Christ, of course, but other tracts of Christian teaching, including the essential names of God, have important work to do. Contra Williams, not only Jesus but created things in general answer the question "What is God?" (see *CHC*, 238). Though the latter do not answer the question as perspicuously as the former, their answer is nonetheless forthcoming. If such is the case, then, one moves beyond a paradoxical account of the Creator-creature relation in favor of a more compatibilist and participationist one.[25] The doctrine of the hypostatic union teaches us that the Son is free to exist humanly, as the one and only beloved Son of the Father, even to death. That the infinite Son, the incarnate Word, the Lord Jesus Christ dies a lonely death, revealing himself "*only* in that which makes no claim to similarity or continuity," is not so much, as Williams claims, "the central theological paradox" (*CHC*, 241). Rather, it is a description of the Son of God's humility in remaining himself in and through an event judged to be utterly incompatible with him. The Lord Jesus remains himself even in death.

Our vocation as Christians is to be assimilated to Christ crucified. When we are united to Christ in baptism and love him in those who are the least, then there is less and less in us that is incompatible with him, the Father, and their Spirit. While I do not quite understand

25. On the compatibilist side of things, see Katherine Sonderegger, *Systematic Theology*, vol. 1 (Minneapolis: Fortress, 2015).

what Williams means by our vocation being a matter of "bringing into being within creation . . . the relatedness of the Word to the Father," the notion of relatedness is nonetheless quite important. Our vocation is to be like Jesus Christ, imitating him in and by his Spirit. Because he has united himself to us, we may be like him, being transformed "from one degree of glory to another" (2 Cor. 3:18).

The hypostatic union is a tract of Christian teaching that is profoundly moral in nature. We are to conduct ourselves like the man Jesus in complete dependence on and openness to the Father and Spirit. Remarkably, the one whom we follow transforms us by his proclaimed Word and the sacramental fellowship of his body. The hypostatic union helps us see how we are to conduct ourselves as those seeking to be indwelt by the infinite life of God that is Christ's gift. We are incorporated through Christ "into the filial relatedness of the Word to the Father" and thereby participate in what is common to the Father, Son, and Spirit (*CHC*, 247).

Doctrine is descriptive—indicative—and imperative in nature. My aim in this book has been to sketch names indicative of God's manner of being in order to show the imperative contained therein. The hypostatic union helps us see that finitude is not the problem, and that the Father's beloved Son is not our rival. Jesus Christ does not come to displace us but to make us new from within through his word and Spirit. Talk of participating in the divine being is, ultimately, talk about imitation of God in "the name that is above every name" (Phil. 2:9).

Conclusion

The Lord Jesus indwells the faithful by his word and Spirit. The faithful cling to him, experiencing his "spiritual embrace" that makes them "fertile with true virtues."[26] The faithful, worshiping and experiencing him, are on pilgrimage, all the while with the help of the angels. The faithful see not only Jesus Christ but also what Augustine calls "the miracles of the visible world of nature." This visible world contains miracles in abundance. It participates in its Creator. To be

26. Augustine, *City of God* 10.3.

with Christ, to be united to his person, is to be united with his sight, to begin to see as he sees. We see the birds of the air with him and hear with him their sermons. The moral character of the hypostatic union comes to the fore, then, with the language of sight. We see with and via him, enjoying in an anticipatory way the bliss that the angels enjoy now "in their immortal blessedness."[27] But when we see with him in joy and all things related to him in joy, we see the cross—we see him "who for the sake of the joy that was set before him endured the cross" (Heb. 12:2). Jesus makes us happy by loving us, a love that takes the form of the cross. And so we die with him so that we might live with him, forever. Jesus comes from God and returns to God, taking us with him, setting us "ablaze with rapture," filling us with a "holy desire" that carries us into "the ineffable and spiritual embrace of God."[28]

We embrace God in this life via imitation. God therefore grants us a participation in himself in and through Christ. We understand the hypostatic union to demonstrate something of a pattern for our participation. The more God pervades us, the more human we become. The man Jesus's inner being is the Word, and he communicates to us all that is his. The result is true creatureliness. To be a creature is to be ablaze with him and all that he is, in common with the Father and their Spirit.

27. Augustine, *City of God* 10.15.
28. Augustine, *City of God* 10.18.

7

Virtue and the Christian Life

Be imitators of God.

—Ephesians 5:1

In her remarkable book *The Architecture of Theology: Structure, System, and Ratio*, A. N. Williams states, "No Christian account of knowledge of God could be accurate or complete without addressing its personal dimension."[1] I concur. What are the personal dimensions? How might we think theocentrically about them? In this chapter I explore further the need to anchor the doctrine of God in our imitation of God issuing in love.

Thomas Aquinas, in his treatise on habits and virtues, helps us think about the personal dimension. He notes in his discussion of prudence as a virtue most necessary for human life that "a good life consists in good deeds. Now in order to do good deeds, it matters not only what a man does, but also how he does it."[2] Similarly, good speech with respect to God matters, as does how we speak, our form

1. A. N. Williams, *The Architecture of Theology: Structure, System, and Ratio* (Oxford: Oxford University Press, 2011), 27.
2. Thomas Aquinas, *Summa Theologiae* (hereafter *ST*) I-II.57.5, in *Basic Writings of Saint Thomas Aquinas*, ed. Anton C. Pegis, vol. 2, *Man and the Conduct of Life* (New York: Random House, 1945), 436.

and voice. In the pages to come I describe the kind of piety that consideration of God's names encourages. The task ahead, then, is to conceive of the doctrine in a way that fosters wonder of God. A devotional frame in concert with virtue is ideal. As Williams notes, "Our understanding of who God is cannot be separated from our understanding of how we go about understanding God."[3] I think that we go about understanding by holy imitation of God "through participation."[4]

Virtue

What God works in us is of himself. In imitating God, we are infused with what is true of God. In leading virtuous lives, we become good—"by it [virtue] something is good." The Christian community is called to live in love, knowing all the while that it is God who causes his love to grow in us. In this connection Thomas writes, "As to those things which are done by us, God causes them in us, yet not without action on our part, for He works in every will and in every nature."[5] God works in us what is of himself but only insofar as we imitate him. Inasmuch as we imitate him are we able to say what is true of him. At this early juncture in the chapter, we see how an account of Christian devotion trades on this remarkable truth: our devotion is ours, and what is ours "God causes," though not without "action on our part."

If God is "the exemplar," as Thomas indeed says God is, following Paul's lead in Ephesians 5:1, then "He must be imitated."[6] But how can we imitate what is God's "very own"?[7] Thomas writes, com-

3. Williams, *Architecture of Theology*, 135. She cites in this connection Gregory Nazianzen, who thinks that only those "who are masters of meditation should write theology" (133).

4. Augustine, *City of God* 11.10. The full quote runs: "The soul itself, even though it may be always wise—as it will be, when it is set free for all eternity—will be wise through participation in the changeless Wisdom."

5. *ST* I-II.55.4, ad. 6 (trans. Pegis, 418).

6. *ST* I-II. 61.5 (trans. Pegis, 473); St. Thomas Aquinas, *Commentary on Saint Paul's Epistle to the Ephesians*, trans. Matthew L. Lamb, OCSO (Albany, NY: Magi Books, 1966), on 5:1.

7. Thomas Aquinas, *Commentary on Ephesians*, on 5:2. Recall the basic teaching regarding divine simplicity. As Augustine notes, "What is meant by 'simple' is that

menting on Ephesians 5:2, "The way to imitate God is in charity." Charity is the key, and we must grow in it. Charity involves progress. In fact, God's charity is "so good," Thomas notes, "that man ought always to make further progress in it."[8] We must advance, but such advancement is God's business. God's goodness, his abundant charity, is the premise.

In other words, imitation involves virtue. To those familiar with Thomas's thought, the language of virtue is well known. The virtues, whether they are moral, intellectual, or theological, dispose "to that which is best."[9] "Nothing is better than God," Thomas comments in relation to Psalm 16:8, and so virtues incline us to God.[10] But, as is also well known, there are acquired and infused virtues. The love with which we imitate the exemplar—God—is his very own. But God is so great and so wonderful that our "proper nature does not suffice for the purpose."[11] Hence God must infuse us with what is his.[12]

If we follow God, virtue follows, which is what Thomas, citing Augustine, calls "*the good life*."[13] God is the subject and agent of the good life. Charity, as a virtue, is preeminent; it is a virtue "directing us to God."[14] This is what gives it its character as a theological virtue. The theological "virtues are called divine . . . because by them God makes us virtuous, and directs us to Himself."[15] The divine virtues by which God directs us to himself enable us to speak of him. Virtue is the path that the doctrine must take. These virtues are not a secondary dimension to the doctrine of God but the means by which God moves us to himself in order that we may not speak falsely about him.

---

its being is identical with its attributes, apart from the relation in which each person is said to stand to each other." *City of God* 11.10.

8. Thomas Aquinas, *Commentary on Ephesians*, on 5:2.

9. *ST* I-II.56.1 (trans. Pegis, 420).

10. See Thomas Aquinas, *Commentary on the Psalms* 15, trans. Hugh McDonald et al., available at http://hosted.desales.edu/w4/philtheo/loughlin/ATP/index.html.

11. *ST* I-II.56.6 (trans. Pegis, 427).

12. I will address the setting of such an infusion when I consider the church in the conclusion.

13. *ST* I-II.61.5 (trans. Pegis, 473). Thomas is citing Augustine's *De moribus ecclesiae catholicae* 1.6 (PL 32:1314).

14. The other theological virtues are faith and hope. See *ST* I-II.62.1, s.c. (trans. Pegis, 475).

15. *ST* I-II.62.1, ad. 2 (trans. Pegis, 476).

The apophatic note in all of this is important to sound. The object of the doctrine of God—namely, God's being and manner of being—far surpasses us. Thomas writes that God "is a happiness surpassing man's nature, which man can obtain by the power of God alone, by a kind of participation of the Godhead."[16] God makes it possible for us to obtain him, and the way we obtain him is via participation. Description assumes participation, and all that by God's power. The happiness of God, in other words, is an ongoing presupposition for our inquiry. God in his happiness makes us virtuous. Hence we must imitate him in charity, hopeful that the charity he supplies us with enables us to obtain him.

Such imitation also serves as a bulwark against idolatry. The love in which we are to live and to imitate surpasses our nature. Though God's love does not contradict our nature, it is distinguished from it. God's love is not ours by nature: though God is his love, we have his love only by participation through imitation. The love of God that we are to imitate is not in us, even inchoately. The charity by which we are directed to God is "entirely from the outside."[17] Accordingly, a foundational truth the doctrine of God unfolds is our great helplessness before the Lord. God must bless us with the charity in which we seek him. If we lack such charity, we will only speak of ourselves. Let us pray that we might acquire charity.

To imitate God by living in love implies "a certain mutual return of love, together with mutual communion."[18] The Christian life is a life of returning love to God and of growing in mutual communion with him. Teaching on God should encourage "a certain familiar colloquy with Him"; it should encourage Christian life. Our colloquy with God "is begun here, in this life, by grace, but will be perfected in the future life by glory."[19]

The Christian life sets out in faith and hope, reaching its perfection in the life to come with charity. Thomas does not conflate charity with the love that God is, but rather describes it as "that love of God, by

16. *ST* I-II.62.1 (trans. Pegis, 476).
17. *ST* I-II.63.1 (trans. Pegis, 483).
18. *ST* I-II.65.5 (trans. Pegis, 503).
19. *ST* I-II.65.5 (trans. Pegis, 503). Thomas cites two New Testament scriptures in making this point, 1 John 4:16 and 1 Cor. 1:9.

which He is loved as the object of beatitude, to which we are directed by faith and hope."[20] Charity is the love with which God is loved. The consequence of this teaching on God is quite important. When we consider what we are to imitate in God, the first thing we say is love. Love is most closely related to the third of the three theological virtues, charity. We imitate neither the faith of God nor the hope of God, for it is nonsensical to speak of both. Instead, we live in love, for love, unlike faith and hope, assumes no imperfection. God is love. In God there is no lack and nothing to want, as there is in us. Faith and hope are gifts given to us by God that direct us to our last end, which is God, who is love itself.

The "personal dimension" of the doctrine of God is at this point strikingly apparent.[21] Because God is above us, the purpose of indicating, however dimly, God's names, his manner of being, is not so much to foster knowledge. Following 1 John 4:16, we unfold names so as to encourage love, specifically the perfecting character of God's love. "Love," notes Thomas, "is perfected by the lover being drawn to the beloved." Loving God is, accordingly, "more excellent" than knowing God.[22] Thus, it is to the benefit of an account of God's names that it be pursued in such a way as to sow love. Love is the most perfect of the virtues—"The greatest of these is love" (1 Cor. 13:13).

There is a deeply trinitarian logic to all of this. The Father does not simply know himself in the Son and vice versa; the Father and Son also love each other in the Spirit. To talk about knowing God without loving God is to detach the Word from the Spirit, the love of the Father for the Son and the Son for the Father. Just as the intellectual and affective are one in God, may they be one in us. The one God is Word and Spirit. The Lord wills to be known and, ultimately, loved. The intellectual is concomitant with the affective. The Spirit whom Christ gives "without measure" leads to Christ (John 3:34). The object of the virtue—God—is one to whom we must be conditioned. As Gilles Emery says of Augustine, contemplation of the truth "needs an *exercitatio*, a conditioning of the spirit which renders

20. *ST* I-II.65.5 ad. 1 (trans. Pegis, 503).
21. Williams, *Architecture of Theology*, 27.
22. *ST* I-II.66.6 ad. 1 (trans. Pegis, 515).

it capable of looking at the light."[23] An account of God's existence and manner of existence, his perfection, and so on, as sketched in previous chapters, is just such an exercise.

God abides in those who love and imitate him. Those who abide in the Spirit abide in the Father, and the Father abides in them through his Word (cf. 1 John 4:16). *Exercitatio*, the elevation of our spirit by the Holy Spirit, however halting it may be, is the ongoing presupposition of theology. Virtue facilitates knowledge that yields to love. We unfold names like immutability "in order to elevate their [i.e., our] minds to the contemplation of God."[24] A life rich in the theological virtues is not so much interested in describing God. Description, as with knowledge, is fulfilled in love—or, you could say, perfected in contemplation. We turn now to Karl Barth in order to see how he encourages intimacy with God and the impact of that intimacy on the Christian doctrine of God. In considering Barth, we see more clearly the strengths of Thomas's account.

Theological Existence

If we are to contemplate God, we must become a certain sort of people, people of virtue, of faith, hope, and love (2 Pet. 3:11). Karl Barth understands something of this; we may learn from him. Accordingly, I think it wise to look at Barth's insights regarding "theological existence," though I press them in a more consistently theocentric and affective direction. Barth anticipates what sort of persons we must be if we are to be stewards of the mysteries of God.

The first dimension of theological existence, Barth notes, is "wonder," the second "concern," the third "commitment," and the fourth "faith." He writes, "We must ask how theology encounters a man (to use the terminology proper nowadays) and how it confronts him, enters into him, and assumes concrete form in him."[25] Barth's concern is with how one becomes preoccupied with God. His instincts are

23. Gilles Emery, "Trinitarian Theology," in *Trinity in Aquinas* (Ypsilanti, MI: Sapientia, 2003), 12, 13.

24. Emery, "Trinitarian Theology," 39.

25. Karl Barth, *Evangelical Theology: An Introduction* (Grand Rapids: Eerdmans, 1979), 63. Pages are hereafter cited in the text.

profitable. Barth recognizes that theology encourages "a quite specific *astonishment*" (64). Astonishment, indeed wonder—these things, Barth avers, form "the sound root of theology" (65). Wonder is anchored in God, and it leads to "concern." "Theological observation of God," Barth continues, "cannot be a genial and detached survey" (75). (Though I am not enamored of the language of "theological observation"—it sounds rather detached—the sense that God cannot be described in a detached way is salutary.) Theological existence is, rather, "the theologian in his existence for himself" (82). The object of theology—God—claims "the most intimate realms of the theologian's humanity" (84). Barth's account of wonder and the concern that it evokes is undoubtedly personal.

This is evident, furthermore, in his description of commitment. It is God who generates and sustains commitment. The Lord God "commits, frees, and summons the theologian to notice, consider, and speak of him" (90). The theologian can speak because of God and make "progress and improvement in theology" (91). The question is how. The answer has to do with virtue. We notice and consider God insofar as we pursue virtue, love. There is great satisfaction to be had in being committed to theology's object, which is also virtue's object. The theologian who remains fixated on God is "a satisfied and pleased man, who also spreads satisfaction throughout the community and world" (95). Though I would prefer the language of "blessed" (the theologian as a blessed person) and "blessing" (the theologian as one who spreads blessing), the instinct is nonetheless helpful. Consideration of God is a delight, and a life of virtue is a life that fosters delight.

Even commitment, however, does not make one a theologian. Faith is, for Barth, the ultimate answer "to the question of what makes a man a theologian" (96). It is by faith that we "move along the path shown him [us] by the object of theological science" (96). Faith is an event, "the indistinguishable condition of theological science," the presupposition of wonder, concern, and commitment. Theological existence, if it is to be genuinely *theological*, poses the basic question: "Will he [the theologian] be a man who is really and effectively astonished, concerned, and committed by the living God—and who thus is fitted for this undertaking?" (105). Theology's purpose is to stimulate astonishment. Virtue prepares us for theology; virtue is how we become "committed by the living God."

Barth's account is not entirely satisfactory. Where I think we need to move beyond him so as to deepen his most productive instincts is with regard to its register. Wonder, concern, and commitment, with faith as their condition, are, in Barth's mind, methodological concerns. Though Barth finds the word *method* "burdensome," he thinks its usage unavoidable. Method defines "a procedural regimen which corresponds to the task of theology" (86). To be sure, Barth would have us become "ever newly surprised" by theology's subject matter (65, 72). Where his account needs supplementation, however, is in terms of its form and voice. Barth's register is intellectual, whereas Thomas's is intellectual and affective. Recall Barth's description of wonder as "but a species of intellectual sensibility" (75). That is true enough, but nonetheless inadequate. I think it important in a treatment of the divine names to hear the word *knowledge* just as much as we do the word *love*. Hence the question that Barth cites with approbation from Professor Tholuck of Halle: "How are things with your *heart*?" We also remember the question Jesus in John 21 poses thrice to Peter: "Do you love me?" (83). Wonder of God, nourished as it is by the wondrous acts of God, assumes an intellectual and affective register. Only then does knowledge give way to love. The aim of knowledge of God is to answer Jesus's question to Peter in the affirmative—"Lord, you know everything; you know that I love you."

The Holy Spirit

Virtue has a deep pneumatological imprint. The Spirit seals us in the Word as the love of the Father for the Word and the Word for the Father. Astonishment gives way to assimilation in knowledge and love. That is the program at hand. What Barth calls theological existence begins, I think, with imitation of God whereby we are elevated and so become more like God. Imitation's end is participation: the Word of God, to use Barth's language, is a "challenge" that "assaults" our autonomy.[26] Yes, but we cannot stop there. The point is to stimulate

26. Barth, *Evangelical Theology*, 96.

a form and voice transparent to the great "I AM WHO I AM" (Exod. 3:14) in order that we may fear him in love. We are fitted for this by believing but consummated in this endeavor by love, "the love with which you [the Father] have loved me [the Son]," love that is the Holy Spirit (John 17:26).

If such is the case, the Christian life has a less episodic flavor than Barth envisages. Barth is fond of saying of faith that it "is a history, new every morning. It is no state or attribute" (103). At the same time, he talks about the need for "progress and improvement in theology" and by extension the Christian life (91). Improvement there must be, but only the kind that is new every morning. When the divine names are pursued in a voice that encourages imitation, we think less in a historical mode and more in a vocational mode. This is not to detract for a moment from the necessity of trusting in God anew every morning. But it is to say that we believe by loving. We imitate God and so are elevated, becoming thereby more like God, "perfect," if you will, following the dominical command of Matthew 5:48, "participants of the divine nature" (2 Pet. 1:4).

There is, in other words, not so much a "procedural regime" corresponding to the doctrine of God. Rather, the doctrine of God is itself a "procedural regime" (86). Its form is prayer and praise; its voice is lament, thanksgiving, supplication, even at times imprecation. Its method, if you will, is that of living "in love, as Christ loved us" (Eph. 5:2). Contemplation of the great I AM is concerned not only with unfolding the riches of, for example, God's goodness but also with how we speak of that supreme goodness. The rich man of Mark 10:17–22 is mistaken in calling Jesus "Good Teacher" not because Jesus is a bad teacher. Rather, he addresses Jesus with too many possessions and cannot therefore recognize God's absolute goodness. Insofar as the man sells what he owns and gives the money to the poor, he is able to speak of Jesus as one whose goodness is exceeded only by his Father.

"Fruitful knowledge of God" and of God's Son—Barth's turn of phrase—is born by detachment from earthly treasures (104). Herein we see the program at work: the divine names evoke fruitful knowledge—that is, imitation leading to participation. The one who would be a theologian is moved "along the path shown him [or her] by the object of theological science" via, in my judgment, imitation of the same (96). And not just a theologian: it is hoped that the Christian, to say nothing of the Christian community, is also moved by God. Love for God is born of and nourished by imitation.

To rehearse this section, faith is perfected in love, the culmination of virtue. Faith is not a name of God, whereas love is. Though I think that Barth shortchanges the affective, he is right to say that "what makes a man [or woman] a theologian" is God (96). Where I think Barth is lacking is with respect to showing how the metaphysics of God encourage imitation of God. The arc of the Christian life is toward one who is being itself, one who is all that he is, one who will be "all in all" (1 Cor. 15:28). Barth attends with great rigor to the demands placed on theological existence by its object. That is salutary. His account, however, would benefit from increased focus on love for God as the highest form of theological existence. In the next section we look more closely at God's love, how growth in that love—in the form of virtue—is a matter of the God-loving life.

God's Renown

We begin to glimpse something of God as we glimpse what God is not. Insofar as we imitate God, abide in God, we see not only *that* God is but also something of *what* God is: love—perfect, infinite, immutable love. As we "live in love, as Christ loved us," we see that God is love (Eph. 5:2). The doctrine of God says not only that God is love but that we are to "live in love" as God's "beloved children" (Eph. 5:1–2). Theology's object determines the form, method, and voice by which theology proceeds. In this section we explore theology with a view to a neglected Hebrew prophet who speaks well of God, Habakkuk.

Thomas notes, quoting Augustine, that God is that "*than which nothing is better or more lovable.*"[27] Nothing is better than God, nothing more lovable. This is the truth that undergirds the God-loving life: "The more perfectly we know God, the more perfectly we love Him."[28] Or, as Williams says, "growth in the knowledge of

27. See Augustine, *The Trinity* 14.9, quoted in *ST* I-II.67.1 (trans. Pegis, 516).
28. *ST* I-II.67.6, ad. 3 (trans. Pegis, 526).

God accompanies growth in love of God and holiness."[29] There is not any competition between knowledge and love, but there is an order. Knowledge is ordered to love and never the reverse.

Whether we are contemplating God's infinity or another aspect of God's manner of existence, an imperative can never be far away. There is an explicitly formational dimension to the doctrine of God. For example, in terms of God's perfection, Thomas notes that "the more exalted the mover, the more perfect must be the disposition whereby that which is moved is proportioned to its mover."[30] There is an indicative truth here—namely, that God is the most exalted mover of creatures. God moves us; we do not move God, contribute to him, as it were. There is also an imperative present: we (creatures) who are movable by virtue of our creatureliness can only be moved toward God to the extent that we become like God—perfect, in other words. To be proportioned—or proximate—to God is to seek a perfect disposition. Insofar as we are perfect, "as [our] heavenly Father is perfect," are we sensitive to the perfection of the one who moves and perfects us (Matt. 5:48). One of the important points that Thomas makes in *Summa Theologiae* I-II.68 (The Gifts of the Holy Ghost) is that "by them [i.e., the gifts] man is disposed to become amenable to the divine inspiration."[31] Gifts move us from outside, thereby rendering us more amenable to what is outside us, God. The Spirit gifts us with virtue, faith, hope, and love, making us amenable to God. Friendship with God, then, is a function of gifts given by God. Our being made friendly to God by his Spirit's gifts, whereby we are elevated and healed of our many defects, is, well, gift. Receipt of the Spirit's gifts, or "abiding habits" as Thomas sometimes calls them, by which we are conformed to the Spirit's direction, sustains Christian life.[32] We are to be appropriately modest before God. We must be "so acted upon by the Holy Ghost" to the extent that there is nothing in our "minds [that is not] amenable to the motion of the Holy Ghost."[33] The Christian life is a life of just such amenability. Without that amenability, our souls are

---

29. Williams, *Architecture of Theology*, 219.
30. *ST* I-II.68.1 (trans. Pegis, 529).
31. *ST* I-II.68.1 (trans. Pegis, 529).
32. *ST* I-II.68.3, s.c. (trans. Pegis, 533).
33. *ST* I-II.68.3, ad. 2 (trans. Pegis, 533); I-II.68.6 (trans. Pegis, 538).

disfigured, turning the beautiful gifts of God into things sour.[34] This friendliness is, again, a gift of the Holy Spirit. There is no room for Pelagianism here. The virtues, as gifts of the Holy Spirit, perfect "the soul's powers in relation to the Holy Ghost their Mover."[35] The Christian life is a life of movement, of being moved by the Spirit with the gifts the Spirit gives us. "Our reason is not sufficient" for searching the depths: the Spirit nourishes the God-loving life. Insofar as we are receptive to the Spirit's gifts, we are "perfected with His gifts that we may obey and follow him."[36] Imitation of God rests on a gift, the gift of God himself. God is the object of our imitation and the one who makes it possible.

Theology is taken up by persons in various degrees of purity. The greater the degree of virtue, the better is the theology. Theology, as with the Christian life, is a fruit of "spiritual sanctification."[37] If theology's goal is to become intimate with the one of whom it speaks, then it must seek the Spirit's mortification and vivification. Prayer is the frame of reference in which theologians think, meditation on the scriptural promises their meat and drink.

Thomas's treatment of the habits and virtues in *Summa Theologiae* I-II.49–70, culminating as it does in question 70 with the Beatitudes, helps us appreciate the importance of "spiritual sanctification." Beatitudes, Thomas notes, are greater than fruits. While a fruit is "something ultimate and delightful," a beatitude is "something perfect and excellent." Christian life requires disposition toward that which is good, and that disposition is, ultimately, a gift of grace. This disposition envisaged is purity of heart that enables one to see God as he is. What could be better or more excellent! Thomas reminds us that a disposition toward that which is supremely good "is effected by love," which is, as we know following Galatians 5:22, the first fruit of the Spirit. Love is the Spirit's "own likeness, since He [the Spirit] Himself is love." Accordingly, an account of the Christian life, anchored as it is in God, will have its principle and end in love, the Spirit who bears us anew.

34. See further Williams, *Architecture of Theology*, 193.
35. *ST* I-II.68.8 (trans. Pegis, 542).
36. *ST* I-II.69.1 (trans. Pegis, 544).
37. Williams, *Architecture of Theology*, 137.

Why then do we write theology? Why sketch such matters as God's essential names? Why write, for example, a treatise on the unity of God's essence and the Trinity of persons, as does Thomas in the first part of the *Summa Theologiae*? We write so that we may be sanctified, that there may be more and more in our intellect and will that is true of God—"therefore be imitators of God" (Eph. 5:1). Let us evermore press toward God, imitate his love by living in love. Let us receive "the whole purpose of God" (Acts 20:27), mindful of its metaphysics and moral consequences. In this regard, Habakkuk's prayer in 3:2–19 is exemplary. When a sketch of the divine names and the Christian life in relation to them is tutored by scriptural genres like Habakkuk's prayer and articulated in a voice sensitive to them, we see how tacit assumptions behind, for example, God's appearing as the brightness of the sun, with "rays [coming] forth" from his hands, remind us that God is in things as their origin and end. As John of Damascus states, God is "participated in by all creation" without the reverse being true.[38] This is the basic truth regarding the God-world relation. "O LORD, I have heard of your renown, and I stand in awe, O LORD, of your work" (Hab. 3:2).

Habakkuk appreciates that God is independent of us, though we are never independent of God. The God Habakkuk addresses is the "Holy One," whose look makes "the nations tremble" (Hab. 3:3, 6). The names of God are enlivened by such a context, a theophanic vision. The personal dimension of the doctrine is not simply, then, the acknowledgment that the disposition of the practitioner matters. There is an imperative, the need for progress, but there is also the description of the divine nature that assumes progress, that there be less and less in us that is not of God, "my salvation" and "my strength" (Hab. 3:18–19). Fidelity matters: saying things that are more rather than less true about God. But such conceptual fidelity assumes virtue: drawing near to God that we may understand and love.

Further to this, Habakkuk speaks of God's renown as he does because he has heard of that renown. He lives and moves, as a Hebrew

38. St. John of Damascus, *An Exact Exposition of the Orthodox Faith* 1.8, in *A Select Library of Nicene and Post-Nicene Fathers of the Christian Church*, 2nd series, ed. Philip Schaff and Henry Wace, 14 vols. (repr., Peabody, MA: Hendrickson, 1994), 9:9b.

prophet, within the orbit of God's renown. The Christian life, similarly, points to God's renown. Habakkuk's prayer is located within the great tradition of God's acts against his enemies, especially the plagues and pestilences that anticipated the exodus. Such acts are demonstrative of God's faithfulness and uprightness, fitting creaturely analogues to promise. Moreover, Habakkuk's rootedness in the great tradition resists an eccentric doctrine of God. Christian life, as with the divine names and doctrine in general, has of course a stable object, the God who as Father, Son, and Spirit is "the same yesterday and today and forever" (Heb. 13:8). Though Habakkuk's reception of the truth of God has an idiosyncratic form—"I hear, and I tremble within; my lips quiver at the sound. Rottenness enters into my bones, and my steps tremble beneath me" (Hab. 3:16)—we are nonetheless wise if we imitate it. Let us emulate such holy fear.

If you are to progress in understanding, then do good and pray. That will help you love the Son (Word) and Spirit (Love) and through them the Father. As Augustine says, following a technical discussion of the mission of Son and Spirit, "If this is difficult to understand, then you must purify your mind with faith, by abstaining more and more from sin, and by doing good, and by praying with the sighs of holy desire that God will help you to make progress in understanding and loving."[39] Faith, Augustine notes, is "a great help for knowing and loving God"; or faith, one of the theological virtues, is indispensable, as is its perfection in love.[40] Without love of God and neighbor, Augustine avers, there is not any knowledge, let alone any sight of God. To make progress in knowing and seeing, we must do good, more and more. The imperative is never very far away. We grow in the good that God "has not acquired," the good with which he is good.[41] Progress in understanding is concomitant with loving what is good and imitating the same. With virtue, we become more like God.

Barth, in his exegesis of Ephesians 5:1 ("Be imitators of God") in *Church Dogmatics* IV/I, notes that in New Testament ethics "we have

39. Augustine, *The Trinity* 4.5.31, trans. Edmund Hill, OP (Brooklyn, NY: New City Press, 1991), 176.

40. See Augustine, *The Trinity* 8.5.13.

41. Augustine, *The Trinity* 15.2.7.

to do with a reflection of the New Testament concept of God."[42] To imitate—the ethical precept—is to reflect God's being and manner of being. Barth recognizes that ethics, the imperative, derives from God, the indicative. This is the consistent pattern of Holy Scripture. Consider, for example, Ephesians 5:8. Christians are, in the Lord Jesus Christ, "light." Scripture tells us something true of God: that God is light. Then Scripture exhorts us to live in a way that is true of God. "Live as children of light." Our call as Christians is to so love God that what is true of God becomes, however faintly, true of us. Jesus does not tell us to become light. He declares, "You are the light of the world" (Matt. 5:14). The present tense in this statement matters—"you are." You are light, and so live as you are. We see the interdependence of the indicative and imperative.

Prayer

There is no greater call in this life than that of the call to prayer. It is the gift that God gives the faithful by which they may imitate and live in him. Prayer is also the gift by which we see. We see through a pure heart, echoing Matthew 5:8.

The call of God to us to pray, to fast, to purify ourselves by abstaining from empty words—this is our training regime. If we purify ourselves by a lengthy abstinence from what is obscene, silly, and vulgar, then we "acquire thereby participation in divinity and become worthy of the grace of prophecy and of the other divine gifts."[43] We become like God.

Our "highest good is to become as far as possible like God."[44] "Likeness to God" is an eschatological goal. We press toward that goal by praying. Likeness to God, though only fully received in the eschaton, is what we must acquire for ourselves, here and now, "by the exercise of his [our] own diligence in the imitation of God."[45] We

---

42. Karl Barth, *Church Dogmatics*, vol. IV/1, *The Doctrine of Reconciliation*, ed. G. W. Bromiley and T. F. Torrance (Edinburgh: T&T Clark, 1956), 190.

43. Origen, *On First Principles* 3.3.3, ed. and trans. John Behr (Oxford: Oxford University Press, 2017), 2:405.

44. Origen, *On First Principles* 3.6.1, quoting Plato, *Theaetetus* 176b.

45. Origen, *On First Principles* 3.6.1.

acquire likeness by imitating, and insofar as we imitate, we pray. We imitate God by loving God and living in love, praying and praising.

We acquire a share in what God is through persevering in prayer. We acquire goodness and life "slowly and one by one."[46] The "habit" of prayer disposes us toward God.[47] The more our lives become prayer "without ceasing" (1 Thess. 5:17), the more we are disposed toward God. This may sound like a heavy burden to some, but rest assured it is not. The yoke of prayer is light and easy. Why? Prayer, as a habit, indeed as the way of virtue, is sustained by its source. The Spirit of the Lord prays in and through us. Prayer is a result of a divine infusion of grace.[48] Left to our own devices, we do not pray and will not pray. Prayer is something that our nature—on this side of the fall—cannot do. And yet, when we pray with God being our helper, we become more, rather than less, human. Prayer is not "contrary to" our true nature.[49] Rather, it is the activity most suitable to it. When we pray, we become who we truly are, children of our Father in heaven.

We could be forgiven at this point for thinking of prayer as either something we do or something that God (the Spirit) does. Fortunately, prayer is not an either/or: either our work or God's work. Instead, we pray, yet God causes prayer in us. We "groan inwardly while we wait for adoption, the redemption of our bodies" (Rom. 8:23). God works prayer in us, but not without "action on our part."[50] We pray in Jesus's name, and Jesus prays through us. As with anything good, however, how we pray matters.

The call to prayer is anchored in God. The triune God is the basis of prayer's intelligibility. Specifically, the Father's vision vitalizes prayer. Recall Jesus's words in Matthew 6:6: "But whenever you pray, go into your room and shut the door and pray to your Father who is in secret; and your Father who sees in secret will reward you." Is it not interesting that Jesus speaks of the Father's sight, not hearing? Is it not the Father's seeing in secret that is prayer's efficacy? God

46. Origen, *On First Principles* 4.4.10.
47. I am using the word *habit* in a Thomistic sense. Habits form us in virtue. See *ST* I-II.49.4 (trans. Pegis, 372–74).
48. Thomas says that this is the case with all "gratuitous virtues." *ST* I-II.51.4 (trans. Pegis, 392).
49. *ST* I-II.51.4, ad. 2 (trans. Pegis, 392).
50. *ST* I-II.55.4, ad. 6 (trans. Pegis, 418).

responds because he sees. And what God sees is prayer undertaken in secret.

If God sees in secret, and if our Father knows what we need before we ask, why do we ask? We ask for our daily bread. We pray for virtue, for faith, hope, and love. In asking we remember whose children we are, children of our Father in heaven. Thus we follow Jesus's example, praying his prayer, in secret. That is our call. We cannot imitate God if we do not pray. When we pray in secret, we begin to see that there is nothing better, nothing more worthy of imitation than God. Prayer reorients our desires in such a way that we begin to desire God, our Father, who is supremely good. Prayer perfects our appetites. We begin to desire, more and more, what is good for us, which is God!

The cross is the center of prayer. The devout hear the call to the cross. "Meanwhile, standing near the cross of Jesus were his mother, and his mother's sister, Mary the wife of Clopas, and Mary Magdalene" (John 19:25). We stand with Jesus's mother, and the two Marys, before the cross. The cross of the Lord Jesus does something supernatural for us. The cross provides us with a new home. Jesus's mother receives a new home from her crucified Son at the home of the beloved disciple. When we die with Jesus Christ, we too receive a new home, a home in heaven in which "there are many dwelling places" (John 14:2). Our new home is full of love, love for him and for his Father and their Spirit. We cannot believe in the reality of our new home too much.

Our call is to come to the light in the light of the Father and the Son. When we come to the light, we begin to see and pray. Once we begin to see in prayer, we begin also to love. We become virtuous. As I have been arguing all along, sight, more so than knowledge, has the greatest biblical density. We see insofar as we love, and we love insofar as we see. Thomas comments, "Love is perfected by the lover being drawn to the beloved."[51] Our love for God grows as we are drawn to God, as dearly "beloved children" (Eph. 5:1). The call of the Christian is to become a lover of the beloved, the blessed and holy Trinity. That is our call, and its form is prayer. Our joy is to "see Jesus," as

51. *ST* I-II.66.6 (trans. Pegis, 515).

the writer to the Hebrews explains, "who for a little while was made lower than the angels, now crowned with glory and honor because of the suffering of death, so that by the grace of God he might taste death for everyone" (Heb. 2:9). There is nothing more loveable than God's humiliated and exalted Son. Nothing is better than him. Let us pray.

This leaves us with a simple question to ask: Does love cause vision or vision love?[52] "Vision is the cause of love." The more perfectly we know God, to say nothing of seeing God, the more we love God. We love God in the love that God is. We imitate God's costly love and so come to participate through prayer in that same love. We "see that which makes them [us] happy."[53] "We do see Jesus," as the writer to the Hebrews notes, and one day we will see his Father, our Father, in the power of their Spirit.

Conclusion

In this chapter, I have shown how integral virtue—the "personal dimension"—is to the doctrine of God. The kind of person we are matters. To be "satisfied and pleased" in relation to God is to make progress in our understanding of him.[54] The doctrine of God is as equally concerned with what we know as with how we know. It assumes virtue. We know the God of the gospel by loving that same God. An account of God's names will proceed in a form and voice that encourages not just knowledge but love as knowledge's perfection. Imitation of God is the way in which we know, fear, and love that of which we, however haltingly, speak. Imitation is the form participation takes. When the theologian is not exercised in prayer and praise by the truths of which he or she speaks, and is not ascending to them via an imitative mode of existence, then there will be much said of God that is not worthy of God. Where God is participated in, however, then Habakkuk's declaration remains on our lips—"O LORD, I have heard of your renown, and I stand in awe, O LORD, of your work" (Hab. 3:2).

52. This is the matter Thomas takes up in *ST* I-II.67.6 (trans. Pegis, 525–26).
53. *ST* I-II.67.3 (trans. Pegis, 521).
54. Barth, *Evangelical Theology*, 95.

We find ourselves joined "to God through love," standing "in awe" of him.[55] "*Purity of heart*," the culmination of virtue—this is the key.[56] Without purity we cannot "acquire participation in divinity and become worthy of the grace of prophecy and of the other divine gifts."[57] The Christian life is a matter of becoming like God. The divine names sketched previously show us something of what this God to whom we are to be like is like. His manner of being is imitable.

Making Christ "loved everywhere" is the highest calling. This is a matter not simply of making him know but of making him loved, and loved everywhere at that. That is the call of all Christians. To know and make Christ known, and to love Christ and to make Christ loved—what a remarkable calling! This is the life of virtue. Accordingly, our joy and duty in this life, however much it may be characterized by hardship, is to "live in love, as Christ loved us and gave himself up for us, a fragrant offering and sacrifice to God" (Eph. 5:2). We live in such love by praying. Our call is to pray without ceasing. Let our whole lives be prayers. Let us love virtue. May we flee greed, fornication, impurity, being careful of how we live, not giving the devil a foothold. When we pray, we become like the one to whom we pray. We become his likeness. I can think of nothing better. And so our call today as Christians is what it has always been, that of loving God and of loving all things in relation to God.

In the chapter to come, we consider the church as the seat of vision. We ask about how God uses it to render us "capable" of him.[58] We shall see the extent to which God uses the body of his Son to make us capable of himself.

55. Origen, *On First Principles* 2.6.3.
56. Origen, *On First Principles* 2.11.7.
57. Origen, *On First Principles* 3.3.3.
58. Origen, *On First Principles*, 3.6.9.

8

Church and the Christian Life

In [the Lord] you also are built together
spiritually into a dwelling place for God.

—Ephesians 2:22

The church is a theological reality. Without recourse to God, our talk about the church will be but "a noisy gong or a clanging cymbal" (1 Cor. 13:1). The church is unintelligible apart from God, and God's written Word, the Scriptures. As the creed reminds us, we believe "in the Holy Spirit" and therefore "one, holy, catholic, and apostolic church."[1] The mystery of the church is understandable only in relation to God.

That much is clear. Our concern in this chapter is to describe the church as the natural home for a theocentric account of the Christian life. Much reflection on the church proceeds as if God were irrelevant. Following Ephesians 2:11–22, especially verses 18–22, we see that the church—"the household of God"—is a creation of the Father through whom we have access in one Spirit in Jesus Christ. The church is God's.

---

1. In this regard, Karl Barth writes, "*Credo in Spiritum sanctum*, but not *Credo in ecclesiam*. I believe in the Holy Spirit, but not in the Church. Rather I believe in the Holy Spirit, and therefore also in the existence of the Church, of the congregation." *Dogmatics in Outline*, trans. G. T. Thomson (London: SCM, 1949), 142.

The church is composed of (formerly) profane persons like you and me. We are, through the cross of Christ, "admitted," as John Calvin writes, "to be members of the same community with Abraham—with all the holy patriarchs and prophets, and kings—nay, with the angels themselves."[2] The household of God includes the patriarchs, the prophets, faithful kings, and discarnate creatures like the angels. The household of God includes the Israel of the promise, the church, and the ministering spirits.

The One Foundation

The church has to learn every day of its only foundation, the promises of God. Idolatry is a perennial temptation for the church. The Old Testament criticism of idolatry is profoundly relevant. Sinners that we are, we not only make God over in our image but we make over the church in our image as well. Scripture is our basis for resisting this move. Scripturally derived categories supply us with the means by which to truthfully describe the church.

The church must allow its life to be shaped by the Old Testament witness as fulfilled in Jesus Christ. The church must see itself in relation to Israel, as an Israel-like people, indeed as "the Israel of God" (Gal. 6:16). The church is where God wills to take up space, visibly, in the world. Unfortunately, as the witness of the Hebrew prophets reminds us, the people of God, especially the leadership of the people of God, do not want to be a dwelling place for God. Without the Old Testament, we are unable to recognize the depth of our infidelity, to say nothing of the great promise of God the Father in Jesus Christ to overcome and destroy it. When our ecclesiology is rooted in the Old Testament, we see the extent to which Israel's life interprets our own. Just as they flee from God, so do we; just as they forget God, so do we. We too resist God's promise and claim: "I will be their God, and they shall be my people" (Ezek. 37:27). No, we do not generally want to be God's people.

2. John Calvin, *Commentary on Ephesians* (2:19), in *The Epistles of Paul the Apostle to the Galatians, Ephesians, Philippians and Colossians*, trans. T. H. L. Parker, ed. David W. Torrance and Thomas F. Torrance, Calvin's Commentaries (Grand Rapids: Eerdmans, 1996), 154.

Accordingly, the body of Jesus Christ must learn, day in and day out, the first commandment: "You shall have no other gods before me" (Exod. 20:3). This is the call of the one God to the one church, to have "the LORD alone." This is something that we must hear. "Hear, O Israel." This is God's word to us too. "The LORD is our God, the LORD alone" (Deut. 6:4). The church, as with Israel, is summoned to hear. Without ears to hear, we will inevitably forsake the one God in favor of idols of our own making. Israel has to learn monolatry, worship of the one God, and the same is true of the church.

The prophets of ancient Israel are our foundation; together with the apostles, they build on the one cornerstone that is Christ. Without the prophetic witness of the Old Testament ruminating in our ecclesiological soul, we have no foundation. We need God, whose words we receive through the prophets. We forget that we are those wandering in the desert, grumbling about God's lack of provision. We ignore the exile, disregarding God's severe judgment on an idolatrous people. We ignore the second petition of the Lord's prayer, "forgive us our sins." The words of the Hebrew prophets to indifferent kings and a (largely) indifferent people are addressed to us too. Insofar as we hear, we are "citizens" with them, who are also "saints." Similarly, insofar as we listen to the prophets, we listen to the apostles. An apostolic church is a church constrained by the Scriptures of the Old Testament (and the New). The foundation that the apostles have laid, as recorded for us in Scripture, is but the fulfillment of the prophets. Christ, "who proclaimed peace to you who were far off and peace to those who were near" (Eph. 2:17), speaks through the Old Testament prophets and completes what they say. A God-centered church is a hearing church.

The one foundation of the church is the one God, Father, Son, and Spirit. To build on God the Father is to build on God the Son, who is never received without the prophets and apostles. Christ Jesus builds us up in himself through them, and that in the power of the Spirit. Jesus is never without his witnesses, the apostles and prophets. They are his voice. Calvin puts it this way: "The Holy Spirit everywhere declares, that he has spoken to us by the mouth of the prophets, and demands that we shall listen to him in their writings."[3] The call to the church is to listen to the prophets and the apostles of God.

The Lord Jesus preaches to us through the prophets and apostles, joining us with him through them. Just as the Father is never without the Son, so too the foundation (the apostles and prophets) is never without "the cornerstone" (Eph. 2:20). That is why we read Scripture, meditate on it, and inwardly digest it. The Scriptures are the word of the Lord, our food and drink, the voice of the living God come to seek and to save. Christ is the center of the Scriptures, the living God himself, uniting both testaments in himself, strengthening us in them through him.

The household of God, with the prophets and apostles as its foundation, and Jesus Christ as its cornerstone, is "a holy temple." Joined together in Christ, "the whole structure grows into a holy temple in the Lord" (Eph. 2:21). Note the word "holy." God's new society, the church, is to grow into something holy. It is exhorted to be holy, "the place where God's glory dwells (Ps. 26:8)."[4] God is one, and God is holy. The people of God are to grow "into a holy temple in the Lord." This is an exhortation. However, this exhortation may be obeyed only in the Spirit—"you also are built together spiritually" (Eph. 2:22). The Spirit indwelling us makes us into a temple. This is not *our* work, but the Spirit working in and through us. God desires to build the church into his dwelling place.[5]

The eschatological character of the new humanity in which God dwells is important to remember. As any casual reader of the New Testament will know, the church's existence is at times—often?—a travesty. See 1 Corinthians 5. The church's often-tragic existence must not detract from what God wills to do with the church. God intends the whole structure to be joined together with reference to Christ. The two groups—Jews and gentiles—are to be one in him and are called by him to grow into a holy temple. Even in situations of exile,

---

3. Calvin, *Ephesians*, 243.

4. Karl Barth, *Church Dogmatics*, vol. IV/2, *The Doctrine of Reconciliation*, ed. G. W. Bromiley and T. F. Torrance (Edinburgh: T&T Clark, 1958), 629.

5. In a strict sense, Paul is speaking eschatologically. The church community, which is to grow into a holy temple in the Lord, has an "eternal form from which is still hidden and awaits a future manifestation." Barth, *Church Dogmatics* IV/2, 630.

the Lord never allows his church to grow entirely alien to him. Even in the midst of rampant apostasy, the Lord calls his people to faithfulness on the basis of the promise.

Though the church's existence is often ludicrous, as was ancient Israel's, "the covenants of promise" (Eph. 2:12) remind us that God's gifts and calling are "irrevocable" (Rom. 11:29). God promises to build in the Spirit a household of Jews ("the original stem") and gentiles ("ingrafted branches"), one that does not know of any divisions, as "a dwelling place" for him.[6] The church is God's household, God's dwelling place, jointed together in Christ, growing into a holy temple.

God calls the church to grow. So often, as the Hebrew prophets attest, our existence is compromised; we do not accept God's call to grow and become what we are in Christ. We are worse than the pagans at times. See again 1 Corinthians 5. We act as if the dividing wall were still intact. If Jesus Christ has broken the dividing wall, reconciling Jews and gentiles in his flesh, how much more has he put to death hostility between us?

Let us ruminate on this. If "the infinite antithesis between God and humanity" has been abolished in Christ, how much more, as Barth notes, have "all *smaller* antitheses" been abolished?[7] Accordingly, the plight of all must be seen in Christ, in light of God's promise to make in Christ "one new humanity." "Consequently," Barth notes, "the apparently absolute antitheses that divide us are revealed to be relative."[8] Without the apostles and the prophets as our foundation and Christ as our cornerstone, we may be tempted to think that we are safe from the world's intrusions. We may be tempted to think that we know greater dividing lines than that of Jew and gentile.

A Fruitful Death

The Hebrew prophets remind us, as do the apostles, of the enmity of God's own people toward God. Apostasy is a tragic possibility for the

6. Karl Barth, *Church Dogmatics*, vol. IV/4, *The Doctrine of Reconciliation*, ed. G. W. Bromiley and T. F. Torrance (Edinburgh: T&T Clark, 1969), 84.
7. Karl Barth, *The Epistle to the Ephesians*, trans. Ross M. Wright (Grand Rapids: Baker Academic, 2017), 140.
8. Barth, *Ephesians*, 141.

Christian community. The Lord is, however, not held hostage by our apostasy. The promise of Christ to build his church stands. Christ's death is "fruitful," despite whatever "melancholy desolations" may befall us.[9] Though God would build us "together spiritually into a dwelling place" for himself, the Lord may have to allow us to spend a great deal of time (multiple generations?) wandering in the wilderness. We gentiles have to remember that we were once far off, "having no hope and without God in the world" (Eph. 2:12). But God delights in raising the dead. God raised Jesus. Exile is not the last word for the people of God, for there is "the story of Pentecost."[10] Israel's history culminates in Pentecost, not exile. The church, like the Israel of old, recognizes that the Lord may also hide his face from us "because of all their wickedness" (Jer. 33:5). As the Book of Common Prayer (BCP) has us pray, "There is no health in us." We are no different from ancient Israel.

And yet the Lord, "whose property is always to have mercy," also as the BCP says, promises "recovery and healing" and "prosperity and security" to a repentant people (Jer. 33:6). Indeed, I think the current travails of the church in the "West" must be read through the prophets and apostles and that of their cornerstone. They are calling us to repentance. The prophets and apostles would have us acknowledge "our manifold sins and wickedness" (BCP). We are guilty and have sinned, but God is always merciful. The Word is at work calling us to purity through pious living.

Jesus Christ "is a Saviour common to both" Jews and gentiles and, remarkably, "he now speaks to them as companions in the gospel."[11] Calvin comments accordingly, "The gospel is the message of *peace*." The gospel gives "peace and calmness to the conscience, which would otherwise be tormented by distressing alarm." Calvin continues, "Take away the gospel, and war and enmity continue to subsist between God and men."[12] They subsist because we worship ourselves rather than delighting in God. Without God, nothing

---

9. John Calvin, *Institutes of the Christian Religion*, trans. Ford Lewis Battles, vol. 2 (Philadelphia: Westminster, 1960), 4.1.2.

10. Barth, *Church Dogmatics* IV/4, 323.

11. Calvin, *Ephesians*, 240.

12. Calvin, *Ephesians*, 241.

that we say about the church, its head, and his many benefits holds good.

Christ is the Savior of all people and in himself makes us his friends. The Lord also makes friends between us. Without Christ, war and enmity subsist between peoples. There is only one foundation for the church, and that is Christ, and Christ is of God. "He alone supports the whole church. He alone is the rule and standard of faith."[13] Christ unites Jews and Gentiles, indeed all people, to himself. Each moment is a gift in which we "who are not united in faith and love" are given the opportunity "to *grow in the Lord*."[14] The building to which we belong is the temple Paul envisages, the temple of God. We are to imitate God. The gift of profound dislocation in a society that cares little about the church, to say nothing of God, is that of discovering our Lord anew, and of reuniting with another in faith and love of God.

I would encourage us to begin again by believing and to press toward the heavenly city. Progress in the faith follows unity in the faith. Let us begin by believing once again the prophets and apostles and their cornerstone. The prophets and apostles are our teachers: they promote Christ. The apostles do not render the prophets superfluous. Each teaches the only foundation, promotes the same object. "We must now orient ourselves accordingly."[15]

The church in the modern world has worked very hard to lay foundations other than the one by which the whole is supported. We are like the gentiles, those "who were far off." The gift of this God-given moment is recognition of our being gentiles. Were we like the circumcision—"the Jews"—we could at least be considered "those who were near" (Eph. 2:17). But, alas, we are not—we are "strangers and aliens." Let us confess that. But let us in the same breath confess that we are "no longer" such (Eph. 2:19). Let us turn to God and God's Son. We learn through the church's preaching and sacraments that God is our goal, and that God's Son, who is God and man, is, as Augustine says, "the goal . . . [and] the way."[16]

---

13. Calvin, *Ephesians*, 243.
14. Calvin, *Ephesians*, 245.
15. Karl Barth, *Church Dogmatics*, vol. III/4, *The Doctrine of Creation*, ed. G. W. Bromiley and T. F. Torrance (Edinburgh: T&T Clark, 1961), 323.
16. Augustine, *City of God* 11.2.

The church's history is Israel's history. We say no to God, and God says yes to us for the sake of "the covenants of promise" made to Israel (Eph. 2:12). Let us listen to the Holy Spirit speak through the mouth of Paul. Let us increase in holiness and in the Spirit. May we by grace become something that more closely resembles the temple of the Lord, a spiritual "dwelling place for God" (Eph. 2:22). May we be a place where God is imitated, his likeness found. Though the form of that dwelling is ultimately eternal, let us become a people who are more and more transparent to the eternal. Let us long to be—here and now—a dwelling place for God. Of all things visible and invisible, "the greatest is God."

However, as Augustine reminds us, God's existence is not a matter of "observation" but of "belief."[17] The church is a believing body— "remember that at one time you were Gentiles by birth" (Eph. 2:11). How do we remember what we were? By becoming a certain sort of (corporate) person, indeed a certain sort of ecclesial person. Let us as a church develop a memory, the memory of what we are without God, "Gentiles by birth." Such a meaning is intrinsic to our pilgrimage. The church, as with the individual Christian, is "on pilgrimage in a strange land."[18]

Not surprisingly, to understand our pilgrimage is to understand God. God "is identical" to his attributes.[19] He is his infinity, his perfection, and so on. The church's pilgrimage is toward its head, Jesus Christ, and in him toward God (the Father). God has never had to become God, whereas our pilgrimage is a matter of becoming what we are in Jesus Christ. We are highly wayward creatures. However, when Christ shapes our lives within the context of the preaching and sacraments of the church, we live into what we have in Christ.

The New Testament frequently exhorts us to become what we are in Jesus Christ. But in and of ourselves we tend to lapse back to what we were. Take the case of 2 Peter 3:11. We are therein reminded of the coming day of the Lord, God's final judgment, when the wicked and their deeds will be made known and judged accordingly. In this

---

17. Augustine, *City of God* 11.4.
18. Augustine, *City of God* 11.9.
19. Augustine, *City of God* 11.10.

light Peter asks, "What sort of persons ought you to be in leading lives of holiness and godliness?" The Holy Spirit is declaring this question to us. What sort of persons are we? Are we persons of the peace of Christ? Do we remember that we "were at [one] time without Christ"? Or do we recognize that in Christ we have been "brought near" (Eph. 2:12–13)? Do we see that Christ restores the likeness of God in us? In Christ we gain a share in God's simplicity, God who "*has* life" and "*is* life."[20]

The sorts of persons we are to become are those who hear the apostle afresh, leading lives of holiness and godliness. Second Peter 3:14 tells us that "while you are waiting for these things, strive to be found by him at peace, without spot or blemish." Yes, strive to be found by him at peace. Christ is our peace. We are to become persons of peace—not any old kind of peace, but the costly peace of Christ. The sorts of persons who are at peace are those who remember what they were. Such persons also recognize what they are. We have in Christ been made what we were not: people of prayer.

The church does not enable participation in God but is where we hear the good news and its myriad benefits through which we share in God. The church does not set us free from eternity; God does. But God brings into being the church, God's people, in order that we may hear and receive the news that makes "wise through participation in the changeless wisdom."[21]

A theocentric account of the church is really parallel with that of the Christian life. There is one foundation, the prophets and apostles, and if we are like ancient Israel, which we are, we often build on a foundation that is not real, that is not of God. We assume dividing walls that Jesus Christ has struck down. We sin and rebel against God. We have lived as those without "hope and without God in the world." God is good. Our God and Father has given us in this moment the opportunity to become less alienated "from the commonwealth of Israel," less unfamiliar with "the covenants of promise" (Eph. 2:12). He gives the opportunity to build afresh on the only foundation that lasts, "the apostles and prophets, with Christ Jesus himself as the

20. Augustine, *City of God* 11.10.
21. Augustine, *City of God* 11.10.

cornerstone" (Eph. 2:20). The Lord in his great grace gives us the gift—the gospel—whereby we become what he is through participation in his changeless nature.

The Grace of Prayer

What Herbert McCabe says of Jesus is instructive. McCabe writes, "He is not just one who prays, not even one who prays best, he is sheer prayer."[22] The church belongs to Christ through praying in the Spirit. Again, as with the Christian life, a theocentric account of the church attends to prayer. In learning to pray in Christ and through Christ, we appreciate the extent to which the church "is the work of grace, that is to say the initiative is from the Father drawing us into communion with his Son."[23] In and of ourselves, we cannot pray: we do not even want to pray. Similarly, the church often disbelieves the gospel. The key, then, is to "admit to our shabby infantile desires." Insofar as the church does so, it absconds from the age-old attempt to create itself in its own image. When we admit that our desires have been rather shabby, "then the grace of God will grow in us, it will slowly be revealed to us, precisely in the course of our prayer."[24] When God prays in us, we learn to want the right things. We learn to want God.

The church is where we learn to "recognize ourselves for what we are." This is what the Father requires of us. He will grow us in himself when we learn to want him. Growth in the gospel is God's work all the way down. The Lord "grant[s] the increase."[25] God is that good, so supremely good, that he grants increase, even to those who receive him at the last hour. The Lord has called us to see that we are a people wandering in the desert, a people taken into exile for our embrace of idols. As a people in the desert and in exile, all of which is of our own making, we have been given a profound gift. That gift is to waste time praying and indeed praising. We are given the gift of time, time in which we may become all that God is "through

22. Herbert McCabe, *God Matters* (London: Continuum, 1987), 220.
23. McCabe, *God Matters*, 221.
24. McCabe, *God Matters*, 224.
25. McCabe, *God Matters*, 224.

participation in the changeless wisdom."[26] Hallowing God's name is the ultimate time waster. It is what is demanded of those who would "become spiritual Israelites and God's people."[27] God is love. The life of the blessed Trinity "is not like the life of the worker or artist but of lovers wasting time with each other endlessly."[28]

Long before there was a world, a cosmos, a universe, there was God, Father, Son, and Spirit, three delighting in one another "uselessly." Prayer is the gift by which we enter into "this worthless activity."[29] God grows us, through Word and sacrament, in the love that he is. By praying, "we become spiritual Israelites and God's people."[30] "Spiritual Israelites" know that they are debtors; they know that God in Christ has assumed their sin and death and healed them of it. They know that God is quite happy to bring forth praise from stone. What we are is not pretty, but it is God who grows and God who grants increase in what is his to those who waste time praying. We learn to want the most important thing, and that is God.

Conclusion

As with the Christian life, so with the church: to understand it we must talk of the being and activity of God. God is identical to all that he is, his attributes. In his great works of nature and grace, God gives us a share in what he is, eternally. The Christian life and the church as its home—these are God's doings. The gain to an account of the church that takes God seriously is quite simple. Ecclesiology's principle is God. Paul's letter to the church in Ephesus reminds us of God, of God's work of making the new humanity. This is God's doing all the way down. God does it in such a way that he draws us to the body of his Son, in whom we become what he is through participation in all that is changelessly his.

26. Augustine, *City of God* 11.10.
27. St. John of Damascus, *An Exact Exposition of the Orthodox Faith* 4.10, in *A Select Library of Nicene and Post-Nicene Fathers of the Christian Church*, 2nd series, ed. Philip Schaff and Henry Wace, 14 vols. (repr., Peabody, MA: Hendrickson, 1994), 9:79b.
28. McCabe, *God Matters*, 225.
29. McCabe, *God Matters*, 225.
30. John of Damascus, *Orthodox Faith* 4.10.

Conclusion

This book has been a pleasure to write. I hope that it has encouraged the reader to consider how God's existence and manner of existence, his perfection, infinity, and immutability, enrich understanding of the Christian life. Moreover, a theocentric account of the life of the believer opens up a space for considering how related themes such as the hypostatic union and the church benefit from contemplation of God's manner of being.

Theology is a descriptive and prescriptive undertaking. It not only describes the mystery of God revealed in the Holy Scriptures but also promotes the movement of the heart, soul, and mind toward God.[1] I have unfolded some of the names of God—those often considered to be the most abstract and remote from the life of faith—so as to subvert such an erroneous view. One cannot consider the sublime truths of God without being engaged by them. There is no room for objective detachment. God cannot be understood without being loved. The state of one's soul—this is not something that can be elided.

This is not to say that precise thinking isn't relevant. By no means! Rather, steadfast scriptural attention to God is "a moral and spiritual discipline."[2] Theology, says Andrew Louth, "is the *kind* of study" that

---

1. See Andrew Louth's wonderful account of theology in *Discerning the Mystery* (Oxford: Clarendon, 1989), 2. He writes against any "division between theology and spirituality . . . between thought about God and the movement of the heart towards God."

2. Louth, *Discerning the Mystery*, 57.

must be pursued prayerfully. Prayer is "the amniotic fluid in which knowledge of God takes form."[3]

Description of God is a moral and spiritual undertaking. We make claims about God's nature, being, and manner of being. And yet we make them within the context of prayerful attentiveness to Jesus Christ and his fulfillment of the promises made to Israel. Articulation of God takes an imitative and participatory form. We grow in likeness to God as we pray, living a life "of loving devotion to God and loving care of our neighbour."[4]

There is no place for moral and spiritual laxity here. Those parts of Scripture that the lectionary expunges are most relevant. God deplores certain acts and thoughts, commends others. Theology as it attends to God stimulates attention to the whole of the canon. We see that the people of God are called to be holy, loving God and one another in relation to God.

Form matters. Doctrinal matters such as God's names—names that express, however obliquely, what God is and how—are formative. We are formed by the majestic and terrifying purity of God by praying, confessing, praising. Consideration and contemplation of God's life is "a way of life."[5] What teachers of the ancient catholic church like Basil remind us of is the need to "become spiritual" ourselves.[6] When we are spiritual, we have confidence, confidence that Scripture's God is knowable and loveable. When we are spiritual, we understand the mysteries, apprehend things invisible, and repudiate "the ruler of this world" (John 14:30).

Indeed, what such a study as this sensitizes one to is the level of traffic between heaven and earth. The patriarchal narratives, for example, are replete with language of the Lord's intimacy with and presence among his elect. See, for example, Genesis 18:1–15. The Lord speaks and is spoken to; his "envoy" speaks his words.[7] The I AM is

3. Louth, *Discerning the Mystery*, 65.
4. Louth, *Discerning the Mystery*, 65.
5. Louth, *Discerning the Mystery*, 86.
6. Basil, *On the Holy Spirit* 9.23, trans David Anderson (Crestwood, NY: St Vladimir's Seminary Press, 1989), 44.
7. "Envoy" is Goldingay's translation of what the NRSV, for example, refers to as an angel. John Goldingay, *The First Testament: A New Translation* (Downers Grove, IL: IVP Academic, 2018), 15.

profoundly close to a people struggling with monolatry. What Basil and others recognize is that the "God-loving life" gives us "a place in the choir of angels."[8] We sing with them and pray for protection from those who oppose their Creator and his people, worshiping the false rather than the true God.

Though we are made "for a little while lower than the angels," our perfection in Christ and the Spirit renders us to some extent superior (Heb. 2:7). We receive via the Spirit the same "endless joy" that they have "in the presence of God." Unlike them, however, we, as a result of Christ's sacrifice once and for all, enjoy "becoming like God, and, highest of all desires, becoming God." Our intimacy with God and all things in relation to God has its apex in "becoming God."[9]

In imitating God, we become like God. Insofar as we become like God, we also become ourselves, creatures made in God's image and restored to his likeness in Christ. Our manner of being as creatures becomes entirely transparent to his, in ever-increasing intensity throughout eternity. There will be nothing in us that is not of him. We shall see. Because God is inexhaustibly good, we shall never tire of seeking and praising him in the company of the angels.

There may be readers who, familiar with Luther's theology, have wondered whether in all of this there is not a whiff of a so-called theology of glory. This is the attempt of theology, more specifically the theologian, to bypass the cross of Christ. I hope not. I have sought in this book to characterize my efforts with a childlike innocence. Such innocence springs from the cross of Christ. We have to be like him if we are to be with him and see him and the Father. When we die with him, we are raised with him to a vision of the Father and to a participation in the nature common to him and the Father and their Spirit. The child is inarticulate, and what I have sought to be inarticulate about is the "how," the details, as it were, of our sharing in the divine life. What I have is confidence that God who delights in working through scandalous means can render us fit for himself throughout eternity, and that through the cross.

8. Basil, *Holy Spirit* 9.23.
9. Basil, *Holy Spirit* 9.23.

In a sense, our receptivity to God will always have a cruciform shape. Our Lord, forsaken and abandoned, "gave up the spirit" (Matt. 27:50 DBH). He died in the Father's presence, receptive to the Father's will even to death. His life, as a life of "sheer prayer,"[10] ended ignominiously. But God raised him from the dead, never to die again. His receptivity to the Father is blessed with immortality. He lives as the one he has always been, the Father's beloved in the Spirit.

We live as creatures soon to be glorified, a mystery that we cannot articulate. Just as the Gospels assume Jesus's divinity and equality with the Father, the gospel assumes that we may become what we were not—God. One of the levels of profundity that we considered in our brief reflection on the hypostatic union is that Jesus does not cease to be any less human because he is God. His divinity does not come at the expense of his humanity. Similarly, relative infinity does not obscure our finitude. The finite, as finite, is capable of the infinite. What Scripture inspires is trust, love of the true Lord and hatred of the false Lord. This is the I AM, "the one who got you out from under the labours of Misrayim" (Exod. 6:7).[11] The root of trust is listening. Dogmatic pursuits do not simply call for a response; the pursuit itself is a response. We pursue an account of God's existence, the manner of his existence, and so on because these names are the form of our response. As we argued early on via Origen, the literal gives way to the spiritual. Description, "I am holy," gives way to prescription, "Be holy." This is true in a methodological sense. But Scripture prescribes—"Be holy"—before it says "I am holy" (Lev. 11:44). The latter is assumed, but only by those who participate in holiness.

We are back to where we began. The way of scriptural receptivity to God is the way of prayer. To receive and to consider the scriptural witness of God in all its fullness is to pray—"Hallowed be thy name." Theology's food is Scripture, and prayer in the Spirit its drink. Doctrine/teaching is formative. What I have tried to show, in treatments of matters deemed to be abstract, of little purchase to the life of the believer, is "a unity between theology and prayer and worship."[12] To hear God and to speak of what one hears is a matter

10. Herbert McCabe, *God Matters* (London: Continuum, 1987), 220.
11. Again, this is Goldingay's translation. Goldingay, *First Testament*, 57.
12. Louth, *Discerning the Mystery*, 133.

of faith, hope, and love—that is, theology. Theology is a matter of "*saintly life.*"[13]

God, Israel's God, the I AM, the Lord, and all the essential names identical to him—they foster a life of faithfulness. And they must be pursued so as to commend that life. Theology, if it is indeed *theo*logy, as with the church's preaching, has one burning passion—namely, stimulating "the believing mind combined with a right state of the heart."[14] I have written this book so as to stimulate the mind and nourish the heart. May God in his great grace use these words to encourage imitation of and participation in his life. Amen.

13. Louth, *Discerning the Mystery*, 156.
14. Louth, *Discerning the Mystery*, 147.

Scripture and Ancient Writings Index

Old Testament

Genesis

1:3 8
1:26–28 76
1:27 76
1:31 58
18:1–15 156

Exodus

3:14 4, 15, 133
3:15 15
6:7 158
19:9 15
20:2 39
20:3 146
33:11 15, 24

Leviticus

11:44 48, 158
11:45 52

Deuteronomy

6:4 146

Joshua

24:21 41
24:23 41

1 Samuel

6:12 54

1 Kings

3:3 58

Job

1:11 74
42:3 34

Psalms

16:2 56
16:8 127
26:8 147
34:8 29
36:9 92, 94
53:1 xvi, 3, 6
90:1 24
100:5 79
119:68 79
119:80 47

Proverbs

9:3 xv

Ecclesiastes

7:20 11, 48

Isaiah

55:11 7

Jeremiah

11:3–4 84
20:9 91
21:8 87
22:17 87
22:21 88
23:24 xvi, 62, 66
24:7 90
31:33 87
33:5 149
33:6 149

Ezekiel

37:27 145

Hosea

14:8 114

Habakkuk

3:2 137, 142
3:2–19 137
3:3 137
3:6 137
3:16 138
3:18–19 137

Malachi

3:6 xvi, 81, 88–89
3:6–7 81
3:7 82, 89

Old Testament Apocrypha

Wisdom of Solomon

10:10 xv

New Testament

Matthew

3:17 109
4:1–11 116
5:8 47, 52
5:14 139
5:30 51
5:48 xvi, 43, 84, 133, 135
6:4 51
6:6 140
6:10 93
6:26 8, 48
7:24–27 6
10:37–38 27
10:38 31
11:27 66
18:10 32, 71, 74
22:1–14 52
25:29 53
25:44 73
25:45 56
27:50 158

Mark

9:24 58
9:35 99
10:17–22 133

Luke

6:47–49 6
10:37 38
18:18–23 26
20:36 53

John

1:18 5
3:5 19
3:30 99
3:34 129
4:24 xvi, 18–19, 64
14:2 71, 141
14:6 87
14:17 64
14:23 26
14:26 xiv
14:28 49
14:30 156
15:14–15 96
15:15 99
15:26 xiv
17:26 70, 133
19:25 141
21 132

Acts

7:55 65
7:56 65
17:23 10
20:27 137

Romans

1:18 8
1:20 5, 10, 12, 71
2:15 13
3:9 84
3:9–20 11
3:10 11, 48
7:14–25 26–27
7:15 40
8:3 49, 120
8:23 140
10:17 52
11:29 148

1 Corinthians

1:9 128n19
1:18 49
1:30 21, 23
3:1 76

3:15 65
5 147–48
8:1–3 119
13 74
13:1 144
13:2 50, 95
13:8 61
13:12 69, 114
13:13 129
15 77–78
15:28 xvii, 34, 42, 69–70, 77–79, 134
15:31 111
15:45 71
15:48 77

2 Corinthians

3:7 78
3:18 79, 105, 123
4:6 108
4:7 80
4:16 85, 93
4:17 73
4:18 7n15, 73
5:1 73
5:17 108
7:1 60
8:9 101
11:31 64, 72

Galatians

2:20 22, 45, 107, 113
4:4 107, 120
5:22 136
6:16 145

Ephesians

1:5 120
1:10 72
1:14 73
1:18 94
1:23 76
2:11 151
2:11–22 144
2:12 148–49, 151–52
2:12–13 152

2:17 146, 150
2:18–22 144
2:19 150
2:20 147, 153
2:21 147
2:22 144, 147, 151
4:23 12
5:1 xii, 43, 95, 125–26,
    137–38, 141
5:1–2 134
5:2 58, 127, 133–34, 143
5:8 139
5:18 69

Philippians

2:6 59
2:9 123
3:7–8 57

Colossians

1:15 73
1:28 47
3:3 107

1 Thessalonians

5:17 75, 140

2 Timothy

3:16 xiii*n*6
3:16–17 xiii
6:15–16 91

Titus

1:9 xv

Hebrews

2:7 157
2:9 142
5:8 49, 119
10:1 xv
12:2 124
12:14 60
13:8 138

James

1:8 85
1:17 21, 93, 97
4:8 82

2 Peter

1:4 xii, 23, 133
1:21 xiii
3:11 78, 130, 151
3:14 152

1 John

3:2 72, 94
3:10 108
4:8 80
4:16 128n19, 129–30
4:18 57
5:18 117
5:19 117

3 John

11 120n22

Revelation

21:1 75
22:2 70
22:14 70

Church Fathers

Augustine

City of God

1 85n20
2 85n21, 86nn26–27
4.2 87n30, 88n31
4.3 89n35
4.26 90nn42–44
4.33 92n51
5 92n52
5.9 93n54
5.18 95n60, 99n76
5.19 99n77
5.21 96n63

6.12 100n78
7 100n79
7.19 101n80
7.30 115n5
8.8 115n6
8.15 115n7
8.17 116nn8–9
8.22 116n10
8.25 117nn11–12
9.13 117n13
9.15 118nn14–17
9.17 119n18
9.18 119n19
9.20 119n20
9.21 120n21
9.22 120n23
9.23 120n24
10.3 123n26
10.15 124n27
10.18 124n28
11.2 150n16
11.4 151n17
11.9 151n18
11.10 20n6, 126n4,
    126n7, 151n19,
    152nn20–21, 154n26

*De moribus ecclesiae
catholicae*

1.6 127n13

The Trinity

4.5.31 138n39
8.5.13 138n40
14.9 134n27
15.2.7 138n41

Basil

On the Holy Spirit

9.23 156n6

Gregory Nazianzen

Oration

14.7 23n21
28.18 22n18

Gregory of Nyssa

On the Christian Mode of Life

131   49n17
133   50n18
143   50n19
145   50n20
148   51n21
152   51nn22–23, 57n37
154   51n24

Life of Moses

1.7   8n18
2.49   13n34
2.76   12n30
2.152   13n31
2.166   13n32
2.188   13n35
2.192   14n36
2.217   13n33
2.234   14nn37–38
2.315   15n39
2.318   15n43
2.320   16nn44–46

Life of Saint Macrina

171   53n27
190   53n28

On Perfection

95   43n1, 45n6
99   45n7

On the Soul and the Resurrection

202   53n29
207   54n30
217   54n32
238   56n35
239   57n36
240   57n38
244   58n39
245   58n40
265   58n41
267   58n42
271   58n43

Treatise on the Inscriptions of the Psalms

1.2.15   19n3
1.3.17   29n41
1.4.28   18n1
1.4.30   21n15
1.7.50   24n24
1.7.57   24n25
1.8.77   24n27
1.8.103   30n45
1.8.106   28n36
1.8.110   30n48
1.8.115   30n46
1.8.122   30n47
1.9.115   28n37
2.3.29   28n38
2.3.34   28n39, 29n40
2.4.39   32n54
2.4.48   33n55
2.5.49   33n56
2.6.61   33n57
2.6.64   33n58
2.7.71   32n53
2.8.73   34n60
2.8.80   34n61
2.11.135   35n63
2.11.137   35n64
2.13.186   35n65
2.14.231   35n66
2.14.240   35n67
2.15.260   35n68

On What It Means to Call Oneself a Christian

85   47n10
86   47n11, 47n13
88   48n15

John of Damascus

An Exact Exposition of the Orthodox Faith

1.8   137n38
4.10   154n27, 154n30

The Orthodox Faith

2.3   83n9

Maximus the Confessor

Ambigua

7.1   20nn8–9
7.2   20nn10–11, 21n15, 21nn12–13, 22nn16–17, 23nn20–21
7.3   22n18, 23n19, 23nn22–23, 25n29
7.4   26n31, 27nn32–33, 29n42
42   27n34, 28n35, 30nn43–44

Quaestiones ad Thalassium

6   36nn69–72
17   36n73, 37n74
22   37nn75–78
60   38nn79–80
61   39n81, 39n82
64   41nn88–90, 42n91

Origen

On First Principles

1.1.5   65n15
1.1.6   66
1.1.7   66
1.1.8   66
1.1.9   64n10, 66, 67
1.2.8   67
1.3.4   68
1.3.6   67
1.3.7   67–68
1.3.8   68–69
1.5.5   70
1.6.4   70
1.8.3   70
2.3.6   71
2.4.3   72
2.6.1   73
2.6.3   143n55
2.6.5   74
2.6.6   74
2.11.7   75, 143n56

3.1.22 75
3.1.24 75
3.2.1 75
3.2.5 75
3.3.3 75, 139n43, 143n57
3.4.3 75
3.5.1 76
3.6.1 76, 139nn44–45
3.6.2 77
3.6.3 77
3.6.6 78
3.6.9 78, 143n58
4.1.7 78
4.3.1 79
4.3.4 79
4.4.6 79
4.4.9 79
4.4.10 79, 140n46

Homily on Luke 23:8
in toto: 54n31

Medieval Writings

Thomas Aquinas

*Commentaries on
2 Timothy*
§124 xiiin6

*Commentaries on
St. Paul's Epistles*
§125 xiiin7
§127 xiiin8, xivnn10–11

*Commentary on
Ephesians*
on 5:1 126n6
on 5:2 126n7, 127n8

*Commentary on
Matthew*
5.12.553 45n4, 46n9
5.12.557 44n3

*Commentary on
Romans*
1.6.114 10n23
1.6.115 11n24
1.6.117 5nn7–8, 7n16,
     12nn28–29

*Commentary on the
Psalms*
15 127n10
52 9n20, 10nn21–22,
     11n25

Compendium theologiae
2, 194 73n20

Summa contra Gentiles
2.52 62n1

Summa Theologiae
I.1 9
I.1.1 xiiin5
I.1.2 xivn9
I.1.3 xvn12
I.1.4 xiiinn3–4, 91n46
I.1.5 xiiin3, 91n45
I.1.6 xv
I.1.8 xv
I.1.9 91nn47–48
I.1.10 92nn49–50
I.2 xiin2
I.2.1 6n14
I.2.2 5n6, 5n9, 5n12
I.2.3 4n5
I.3.1 19n5
I.3.2 19n4
I.3.3 20n6
I.4.3 46n8, 48n16
I.6 4n3, 5n11
I.7.1 62nn2–3
I.7.2 63n5, 63nn7–9,
     77n21
I.8.1 88nn32–34,
     89nn36–37

I.8.2 62n4
I.8.3 90nn38–41
I.9 xvn14
I.9.1 81n1, 82nn3–5
I.9.2 82nn6–7, 83nn8–13,
     84n16
I.10 xv
I.10.1 84n17
I.10.2 85n18
I.10.3 85n19
I.10.4 86n22
I.10.5 86n28, 86nn23–25,
     87n29
I.12.2 93n53
I.12.5 94nn56–57
I.12.6 94nn58–59
I.12.11 96n62, 97n65,
     99n74
I.12.13 95n61
I.39.2 72n18
I.39.8 73n19
I.83.1 33n59
I-II.49–70 136
I-II.49.4 140n47
I-II.51.4 140nn48–49
I-II.55.4 126n5, 140n50
I-II.56.6 127n9, 127n11
I-II.57.5 125n2
I-II.61.5 126n6, 127n13
I-II.62.1 127nn14–15,
     128nn16–17
I-II.65.5 128nn18–19,
     129n20
I-II.66.6 129n22, 141n51
I-II.67.1 134n27
I-II.67.3 142n53
I-II.67.6 134n28, 142n52
I-II.68 135
I-II.68.1 135nn30–31
I-II.68.3 135nn32–33
I-II.68.6 135n33
I-II.68.8 136n35
I-II.69.1 136n36

Author Index

Anselm, xvii
Aquinas, Thomas. *See* Thomas Aquinas
Augustine, 20n7, 44n2, 52, 85nn20–21,
    86nn26–27, 87, 88n31, 89, 90nn42–44,
    92–93, 95n61, 96, 99nn76–77, 100,
    101n80, 105, 109, 115–20, 123,
    124nn27–28, 126n4, 127, 134, 138,
    150–51, 152nn20–21, 154n26

Barth, Karl, 45, 106, 130–34, 138–39,
    142n54, 144n1, 147nn4–45, 148,
    149n10, 150n15
Basil, 156–57
Behr, John, 7n15, 64nn11–12, 65n13

Calvin, John, 48n14, 145–47, 149,
    150nn13–14

Emery, Gilles, 129–30

Goldingay, John, 156n7, 158n11
Gregory Nazianzen, 22n18, 23n21,
    126n3
Gregory of Nyssa, xi, xii*n*1, 3–4, 8, 12–
    16, 18–19, 21n14, 24, 28–30, 32–33,
    35nn63–64, 35, 42–43, 45, 47, 48n15,
    49n17, 50–51, 53, 56, 57nn36–38, 58
Griffiths, Paul, 63n6

Hart, David Bentley, 3n1, 4, 5n10, 6n13,
    9n19, 12nn26–27, 25n28, 26n30,
    40nn83–87

John of Damascus, xi, 83, 137, 154n27,
    154n30

Kerr, Fergus, 96n64, 97nn66–68

Louth, Andrew, 155–56, 158n12,
    159nn13–14
Luther, Martin, 34, 157

Mascall, Eric L., 19n2, 24n26, 32
Maximus the Confessor, xi, 18, 20, 22–23,
    25–27, 29, 36–39, 40n88, 41–42,
    110–11
McCabe, Herbert, 153, 154nn28–29,
    158n10
McCormack, Bruce, 45
Murray, Paul, 33n59, 71

Origen, xi, 54, 64–79, 139nn43–45,
    140n46, 143nn55–58, 158

Przywara, Erich, 7n17, 121

Richard of Saint Victor, 59

Sonderegger, Katherine, 84nn14–15,
    122n25

Tanner, Kathryn, 105
Tholuck, August, 132
Thomas Aquinas, xi–xv, 4n3, 4n5, 5nn6–
    9, 5nn11–12, 6–12, 19nn4–5, 20n6,

25, 33, 44, 45n4, 46nn8–9, 48n16,
62–63, 71–72, 73nn19–20, 77n21,
81–83, 84nn16–17, 85–86, 87n29, 88,
89nn36–37, 90nn38–41, 91nn45–48,
92nn49–50, 93n53, 94–96, 97n65,
99n74, 106, 109n3, 125–29, 134–37,
140nn47–50, 141, 142nn52–53

White, Thomas Joseph, 15
Wilken, Robert Louis, 52, 55, 59nn44–46,
60–61
Williams, Anna N., 47, 79n22, 125–26,
129n21, 134–35, 136n34, 136n37
Williams, Rowan, 98–99, 105–11, 113–14,
116–17, 121–23

Subject Index

agency, 88, 108–12
amenability, virtue and, 135–36
angels
  immutability and, 83
  infinity and, 63–65
  participation and, 28, 32–33, 117
  perfection and, 53–54, 157
  worship and, 117
antitheses, the church and, 148
apostles, the, 146–47
asceticism, 14, 33–35
astonishment, theological, 130–32
attributes, God's. *See* names, God's
authentic knowledge, 38

baptism, 36–40
Beatitudes, the, 136
beauty, perfection and, 57
being, God's. *See* names, God's
beneficence, imitation as, 24
birth, spiritual, 36–40
blessedness, life of, 100–101
body, physical, 26–29, 41, 63–68, 77–79

causality, 4, 11
changeless, God as. *See* immutability
charity, 94–96, 127, 129
choice, 74, 83–87, 92–94
Christ
  attributes of, 49–51, 59, 66–67, 87
  the church and, 148–54
  the cross and, 141–42, 157–58
  participation and, 21–23, 105–24

church, the, 55–56, 144–54
commitment, theological, 130–32
composite, Christians as, 109
concern, theological, 130–32
contentment, immutability and, 90–91
creation
  Christ and, 105–24
  existence and, 4–9, 11
  immutability and, 95–96, 98
  infinity and, 76
creaturely immutability, 95–96
cross, the, 141–42, 148–53, 157–58

deification, 28, 37, 94
demons, 89–91, 115–20
devotion, 75–76
discontent, immutability and, 90–91
divergence, immutability and, 93–94
divine sense, 64, 66–67
doctrine, xii, 50–52, 75–76
duality, immutability and, 99

election, immutability and, 83
eschatology, 12, 77–79, 147–48
essence, God's, 10–13, 106–7
eternity, 84–85
excellence, God's, 11, 65–68, 71–73,
  134–39
exercitatio, 129–30
existence, God's
  change and, 25, 32–35
  imitation and, 24–25, 34–36
  knowledge and, 10–16, 19–21, 38

manner of, 18–42
names and, 3–10
participation and, 7, 15–16, 19–23, 35
prayer and, 28–34
virtue and, 21–23, 25–29, 130–32

faith, 53–54, 130–34, 138
familiarity, divine, 26–29
felicity, immutability and, 92
foolishness, 6–17
foundation, God as, 145–48
friendship, God's, 16, 24–25, 96–100, 135–36

glory, theology of, 157–58
God
  and change, 25, 32–35
  essence of, 10–13, 106–7
  existence of, 5, 10–11, 19–21
  as foundation, 145–48
  friendship of, 16, 24–25, 96–100, 135–36
  as "I AM," 6–10, 15
  image of, 46–49, 76
  imitation of, 24–25, 34–36
  incorporeality, 18, 65–68
  immutability of, 91–93
  and infinity, 64–65, 71–73
  knowledge of, 10–16, 19–21, 37–38
  names of, xi–xii, 3–10, 14–17
  participation, 7, 15–16, 19–23, 35
  perfection of, 52–57
  prayer and, 28–34
  promises of, 145–48
  renown of, 134–39
  simplicity of, 18, 25, 31, 126n7
  and virtue, 21–23, 25–29, 130–32
grace, immutability and, 89–90

history, faith as, 133
holiness. See perfection
Holy Spirit. See Spirit, Holy
hypostatic union, the, 105–24

"I AM," God as, 6–10, 15
idolatry, 18–19, 128
image, God's, 46–49, 76
imitation
  Christ and, 121–23
  existence and, 24–25, 34–36

immutability and, 94, 97
  perfection and, 43–50, 57–58
  virtue and, 125–43
immediacy, scriptural, xiii–xiv
immortality, 117–18
immutability, 24–25, 81–101
incarnation, 105–24
incorporeality, God's, 18, 65–68
individuality, 74, 77–79
infinity, 62–80, 98n72
intellect. See reason
intimacy. See friendship, God's
invisibility, God's
  existence and, 5, 10–11, 19–21
  immutability and, 91–93
  infinity and, 64–65, 71–73
  perfection and, 52–57
Israel, the church and, 145–46

Jesus. See Christ
justification, infinity and, 68

knowledge
  existence and, 10–16, 37–38
  infinity and, 66–67
  love and, 119, 129, 134–35

Lady Wisdom, xv
law, the, 87
light, revelation and, 91–92, 94
likeness, God's, 46–49, 76
love
  demons and, 115–20
  infinity and, 64, 73–75
  participation and, 25–29, 94–96, 114–15
  perfection and, 50–51, 60–61
  virtue and, 128–29, 134–36, 142–43

Macrina, Saint, 53
method, theological, 132
model, language of, 98n70
morality. See virtue
Moses, 14–17, 24–25

names, God's, xi–xii, 3–10, 14–17
necessary knowledge, 119
negation, existence and, 11
nihilism, knowledge and, 13–14

obedience, 97. *See also* virtue
Old Testament, the church and the,
    145–47
operation, immutability and, 85–86

participation
    existence and, 7, 15–16, 19–23
    incorporeality and, 65–68
    perfection and, 58
    prayer and, 28–34
    virtue and, 25–29, 38–39, 128
perfection, 43–61, 128–29, 134–36
piety. *See* worship
power, God's, 72
practice, theology and, xii, xiv
praise, 28–29, 32–33
prayer
    the church and, 153–54
    existence and, 27–34, 75–76
    Scripture and, 158–59
    virtue and, 51, 93–94, 139–42
process, virtue and, 133–34
promises, God's, 145–48
properties, God's. *See* names, God's
prophets, the, 146–47
proportionality, 26–27
Psalter, the, 29–32
purity, 8–9, 13, 143. *See also* virtue

qualities, God's. *See* names, God's

rank, social, 86
reason, 11, 66–67, 93
register, theological, 132
relative immutability, 95
relative knowledge, 38
renown, God's, 134–39
residing, participation and, 27
rest, God at, 20–21
resurrection, infinity and, 77–79
revelation, 19, 91–92, 95–96, 122
rewards, Christian, 51–52

sanctification, 68–69, 136–37
satisfaction, immutability and, 90–91

Scripture, xiii–xv, 35, 55–56, 91–92, 145–47,
    158–59
sense, divine, 64
sense perception, 10–11, 13–16, 19–21,
    52–57, 73–74
sent, Jesus as, 49
sight, 66, 71–75, 91–93, 94n55. *See also*
    invisibility, God's
simplicity, God's, 18, 25, 31, 126n7
sin, 8–10, 57–59, 84–88, 148–53
soteriology, virtue and, 23–24
soul, the, 26–32, 53–54
speculation, theological, xiv
speech, existence and, 8
Spirit, Holy, xiv, 64–65, 67–71, 73, 132–34
subjective immutability, 95–96
suffering, Jesus and, 49
superiority, God's. *See* excellence, God's

temple, church as, 147–48
theology of glory, 157–58
Trinity, the, 55–56, 68–71, 73, 98–99,
    129–30

unbelief, knowledge and, 11–12
unchanging, God as. *See* immutability
unmoved, God as, 20–21
unseen, God as. *See* invisibility, God's

virtue
    existence and, 35–40
    imitation and, 50, 125–43
    immutability and, 91–93, 96–100
    knowledge and, 11–14
    participation and, 21–23, 25–29
    prayer and, 28–34

wickedness. *See* sin
will, 74, 83–87, 92–94
wisdom, Scripture and, xv
wonder, theological, 130–32
Word, the, 106–15
worship, 89–91, 95, 99–100, 116–17